"A Child of the Indian Race"

"A Child of the Indian Race"

A STORY OF RETURN

Sandy White Hawk

Foreword by Gene Thin Elk
Introduction by Terry Cross

MINNESOTA
HISTORICAL
SOCIETY PRESS

Portions of chapters 1, 3, and 4 were previously published in "Generation after Generation, We Are Coming Home," in *Outsiders Within: Writing on Transracial Adoption,* ed. Jane Jeong Trenka, Julia Chinyere Oparah, and Sun Yung Shin (Cambridge: South End Press, 2006). Each person who is quoted in Chapter 13 has given permission for use of their words of witness. The words of witness by Racheal M. White Hawk on pages 163–64 were originally published in *Indian Country Today,* November 24, 2012, and have been revised by her.

mnhspress.org

The Minnesota Historical Society Press is a member of the Association of University Presses.

Manufactured in the United States of America

10 9 8 7 6 5 4 3 2 1

♾ The paper used in this publication meets the minimum requirements of the American National Standard for Information Sciences—Permanence for Printed Library Materials, ANSI Z39.48–1984.

International Standard Book Number
ISBN: 978-1-68134-241-2 (paper)
ISBN: 978-1-68134-242-9 (e-book)

Library of Congress Control Number: 2022939083

This and other Minnesota Historical Society Press books are available from popular e-book vendors.

"A Child of the Indian Race" was designed and typeset by Judy Gilats in St. Paul, Minnesota. The text typeface is Loretta from Nova Type Foundry and the display typeface is Halyard Text from Darden Studio.

For Nina LuLu White Hawk, Garneaux,
my Indian mother, the one who gave me life.

....

This is also for all our Indian mothers and fathers. It is for the mothers whose shame kept them from forgiveness of self, who carried the secret that they gave life; the most sacred gift of all.

We longed to hear your voice, feel your arms, and look into your eyes. Our path was this difficult path; a path that is guided in compassion.

For the Indian fathers who were left out of the decision process. For the father who was not even told you had a child, this is for you. You can decide today to be part of the life you helped bring into the world.

To our grandparents who were robbed of the opportunity to hold us and watch the future generations grow to maturity. We wanted your patience; missed your direction and wisdom. Most of all we thank you for your prayers.

So, hear us wherever you are, our Indian mothers and fathers and grandparents.

Thank you for giving us life.

Forgive yourself.

Even if we came into this world in the worst of circumstances.

We are not that circumstance; we were sacred when we were born

separate from the hardship that surrounded us.

Our life is good and has a purpose.

I pray for good health and happiness for us all.

Sandy White Hawk, about 1955

Contents

Foreword

Agliaku: Bringing Them Home

GENE THIN ELK

A HEALING AND INFORMATIVE BOOK like the one you are holding in your hands is like a beacon of light in the historical haze of Indigenous family disenfranchisement, displacement, and slavery. It offers an avenue for many Indigenous people to understand the insidious brutality and inhumanity of genocide directed at their families and nations by colonialist people.

When Europeans invaded Turtle Island, they brought systems to destroy the people they found here. The colonialists' loyalties and actions were born of fear and mistrust. To bolster their beliefs in their own superiority, they used commerce and politically charged religious ideologies to control and manipulate Indigenous people. Their value structures incorporated malign beliefs that established a hierarchy of cultures. They used these beliefs and values to suppress and oppress, regulating commerce and resources. They carried out psychological control: establishing qualifications for their deity's favor among the people they controlled, declaring who was worthy of the deity's discourse. The control seemed complete, and it was comprehensively designed for establishing fear as the primary motivator and for seeing themselves as the privileged class of people!

Through the colonialists' ability to wield this power, to establish systems of control, and to provide favors to those who embraced loyalty to their causes, they came to sincerely believe that they are a superior race of people.

These beliefs were evident in their desire to seek out, conquer, and colonize more of the world. The goal was to acquire more resources, proselytize their beliefs, and subjugate the Indigenous populations—making them take on the invader's culture, but exist in it as a lower caste. Power and greed were the two beasts that needed to be fed to keep the progenitor fear alive. Wars—Holy Wars—became a way of life, and their insatiable appetite of always wanting, needing more, and never being satisfied, became an addiction to their own myths, lies, and religiously sanctioned existence. Their justification for this was the Doctrine of Discovery, based on the Papal Bull of 1493, which declared that any land occupied by "non-Christian" peoples could be "discovered" and taken over by Christian rulers. Essentially, Indigenous people were savages, like animals, only fit to be taken over and made to become Christians. This foundational principle, reflected in the values, genocidal policies, dispossession of resources, and denial of a people's right to be human with the freedom to exist, has continued to underpin the legal systems of colonial powers across the world. And through all these years, the federal and state governments sanctioned the work of "Christian" organizations and churches who dispossessed the Indigenous families on this Turtle Island with the premise of "humanizing" them and giving them a better future. Instead, they took our children.

This book seeks to provide healing paths back toward home in ourselves, our families, our communities, and all Indigenous nations, to be wolakota, a loving member of the universe and Unchi Maka, Grandmother Earth.

Agliaku—bringing them home—gives voice on many levels to those who were unlawfully stolen and used for various religious causes by people with an insatiable appetite for something more than what they have or had. It is based upon natural, supernatural, and Indigenous wichounye woope' (laws of living). The voice is that of a thundercloud rolling and rains pouring, millions of tears washing away at the years and fears, coming home, then finding the beautiful Mother Earth culture of the people, the Indigenous people, the Lakota, Dakota, Nakota, Anishinaabe, Diné, Seneca, and all the people of Turtle Island.

The story of our Indigenous ways is a terrible story made healing by sharing. The early chapters were very beautiful; then others wrote a few pages of hurt, rage, anger, and shame through dehumanization; and now that history will no longer hold us in that chapter! It is a new day, a new season, a new reason to reclaim our Creator-given birthright to shape our destiny, and this book is a beacon to shine a light on the path toward balance!

Hau, hechetu elo! (Yes, that's the way it is!)

Mitakuye Oyasin.

Introduction

The Indian Child Welfare Act and Adult Adoptees and Fostered Individuals

TERRY CROSS
Founder and Senior Advisor
National Indian Child Welfare Association

IT IS AN HONOR AND PLEASURE to write an introduction for this book by a dear friend whose story illustrates why I have devoted my life to reforming child welfare, healing intergenerational trauma, and advocating for proper implementation of the Indian Child Welfare Act (ICWA). Sandy White Hawk's story of adoption and return is rooted in a long and painful history. Her story is compelling, but it is the story of thousands like her. It is a story of the negative consequences of colonization, brutal federal policy, misguided good intentions, and systemic bias. Sandy asked me to write this introduction to provide a broader context, so people would know that her experience is not just an isolated one. To make sense of Sandy's story, I believe the following will be helpful.

Adult American Indian/Alaska Native (AI/AN) adoptees have lived the direct consequences of hundreds of years of colonialism and then federal Indian policy. Their lived experience and survival are a testament to the strength and courage of Indigenous peoples, and most adoptees do not realize the extent to which their personal experience was shaped by a legacy of colonial power and privilege.

Indigenous children have always been used as a means to gain ultimate control of conquered territory. As with taking land and natural resources, the invader gains power by dismantling the institutions of the conquered. Taking away children is a vital part of disrupting the integrity of the family and ensuring power over the colonized. Early in the 1600s, the Virginia Company authorized the kidnapping of Indian children to civilize the local Indian populations (Bremner, 1970). In the 1600s and 1700s, the Catholic Church authorized the forced taking and conversion of children. In 1819, the US Congress passed the Civilization Fund Act, which funded programs to save and civilize the Indian, empowering churches to establish schools and to remove Indian children. In the 1880s, "outing" programs placed Indian children on farms and ranches to "civilize" them (Bremner, 1970). Since the 1870s, federal policies have encouraged the removal of children from their families and communities to off-reservation boarding schools. Children as young as three and four years old were placed in boarding schools and raised without the benefit of family or tradition. The early boarding schools became large military institutions where it was illegal to speak your language or practice your religion. Widespread exploitation and abuses at boarding schools were reported. So great were the problems that in 1891 Congress conducted an investigation, but to no avail. In 1893, Congress authorized Indian agents to withhold rations from families who refused to allow their children to be taken (Kappler, 1904).

As late as 1976, I witnessed a Bureau of Indian Affairs (BIA) boarding school teacher punish two Alaska Natives for speaking their language. They were told to "cut out your dog grunts" and were referred to the principal's office. Adults today who attended these institutions have varying reports. Some found their experience helpful, but most found they no longer fit in their home community or culture, nor could they fit in the white world that rejected them as "Indian." One boarding school alumnus recently told me that her only recourse was to crawl into a bottle for twenty years. Today, having entered recovery, she is helping others whose families were devastated by the removals.

In the 1920s, Congress enacted the Snyder Act of 1921, which gave the BIA broad powers to "protect the welfare" of Indian people, including forced removal of their children without due process. Any BIA worker who believed an Indian child to be at risk could unilaterally remove them from their family and place them in boarding school or in foster care. This practice was the norm through the 1970s.

In the 1950s, this practice became more formalized with the establishment of the Adoption Resource Exchange of North America (ARENA) Project, under which the BIA and the Child Welfare League of America (CWLA) jointly placed hundreds of AI/AN children in non-Indian adoptive homes under the authority granted them by the Snyder Act. This program was reportedly designed to rescue AI/AN children from the impoverished conditions of Indian reservations and to give them a "better life." CWLA went on to train states and private agencies in how to do this, leading to the conditions reported by the Association on American Indian Affairs (AAIA) in the early 1970s. One out of every four AI/AN children was in out-of-home care and 85 to 95 percent were in non-Indian homes and institutions (Unger, 1977). It was not until the year 2001 that CWLA officially apologized to American Indians for their role in this act of cultural genocide. Today, CWLA is a partner in protecting the rights of eligible AI/AN children and families and is helping its member agencies understand their obligations under the ICWA.

The dynamics of power and privilege operated in the federal programs and policies for removal and assimilation. Federal agencies imposed their view of what was needed without regard for the trauma that was wrought on AI/AN families and children. While conditions were harsh in many areas, the removal of children only made the problems worse by compounding them with intergenerational loss and grief. Most adult adoptees of that era knew nothing of why they were placed for adoption, nor were they ever told where they were from or who their family might be. Most lost their rights as citizens of Indian nations and their identities because the policy makers of the time felt they could have a better life by growing up in the white world.

Despite the attempted destruction of the AI/AN family, change would come. In the 1940s, AI/AN leaders who had fought for this country in World War II began to organize. In the 1950s, they fought against termination and increasing state intervention in tribal affairs. In the 1960s, the civil rights movement, the American Indian Movement, and the War on Poverty began to bring attention to AI/AN issues. With the Nixon administration came a reversal in federal Indian policy that was to have a dramatic effect on child welfare and adult Indian adoptees. The new policy of self-determination recognized that Indian tribes were going to continue to exist and that forced, or "humanitarian," assimilation was not working. The new policy recognized that the highest laws of the land, the US Constitution and treaties, obligate the federal government to recognize tribal governance and sovereignty. In essence, AI/AN people would be better governed by running their own affairs.

The Indian Self-Determination and Education Assistance Act empowered tribes to contract with the BIA to run any program offered by that agency. One of the first programs that several tribes contracted to run was social services. As tribes began running social services, they began looking for their children and seeking to bring them home. But states resisted and refused to recognize tribal jurisdiction. Tribes sought the aid from AAIA, which conducted the national study and the advocacy that would lead to the passage of the Indian Child Welfare Act (ICWA) in 1978. Many AI/AN activists contributed to the passage of the act, and some of the most vocal were parents and others who had lost their own children, siblings, or relatives.

ICWA contains two major components. First, it set forth several conditions that states must follow when serving AI/AN children. Second, it reaffirmed the right of tribes to take jurisdiction over their own child welfare matters. Further, it encouraged and supported the exercising of this jurisdiction with grants to tribes and by setting up a process for tribes to establish juvenile courts, codes, and child welfare services. Most important for adult AI/AN adoptees, it created the possibility that they could gain access to critical information that would help them determine their eligibility for tribal enrollment.

The unique legal relationship between the US government and the Indian tribes made it possible for Congress to adopt this national policy. ICWA has been found to be constitutional because it affirms rights based on a political status and not on race. In order to determine if individuals have rights under ICWA, it must first be determined whether they are eligible for membership (citizenship) in a tribe. Adult adoptees often encounter resistance from adoption agencies or states with regard to birth records. However, under federal law, they have a right to have information transferred to the BIA, and that allows the BIA and/or tribe to determine eligibility. Once an adoption agency realizes that they may be subject to a civil rights lawsuit for any damages caused by withholding critical information, their cooperation is usually forthcoming.

Unfortunately, the practice of the unwarranted removal of AI/AN children from their families did not end with the passage of ICWA. In fact, it still continues today. In many cases, ICWA has not been followed, and children who should have been covered by ICWA have been lost. Some AI/AN children who have had their adoptions or foster care handled under ICWA have aged out of the system, only to find that the state or county failed to keep adequate records. They are left with few options for finding who they are. Some have been told that their families are all dead or dysfunctional, only to learn that they have adult siblings or other relatives looking for them. Many adult adoptees or fostered individuals are now making their way home, or being found by relatives, and are working to have their membership status affirmed.

Recently John Talley, an old Mohawk friend and fellow member of one of the Iroquois nations, passed away. I had met him in the fall of 1975 in the lobby of what was then the

Urban Indian Council in Portland, Oregon. We soon discovered that we were both from New York, and—being a long way from home—found an instant bond. He was hungry to hear about my Seneca heritage and to talk of home. He was quick to tell me he did not have enrollment papers because he was adopted at age six or seven by a family in Syracuse. He barely remembered his mother, but did remember his older sister, who was sent away to boarding school when he was taken away for adoption. The only information he had was his sister's admonition to never forget that he was Mohawk. John was an activist, AIM member, radio host, and ardent supporter of ICWA. Some doubted his story. Some even made jokes at his expense, but he never gave up hope. Finally, when he was in his seventies, his family found him. He learned he had many siblings and many nieces and nephews. He learned that his family never gave up looking for him. That year, he spent his first Christmas with family, and a year later was welcomed home on his reservation. Just a year before his passing, we sat together at a community event. He leaned over to me from his wheelchair and said, "You know, I got my enrollment papers. Now nobody can say I'm not Mohawk."

It is impossible to know the power of the impact of identity, but we now have research data that suggests a healthy cultural identity is associated with at least eight positive social and mental health outcomes, from lower rates of depression to higher educational attainment. Sandy White Hawk's story is well told and moving. It provides a window on the negative consequences of misguided federal policies that still reverberate through generations of our people. Today there is a resurgence of interest in AI/AN heritage. Thanks to ICWA, adult adoptees have access to vital information. Like Sandy and my friend John, many are healing from their past traumas and, in so doing, contributing to the wellness of other Native people.

References

Bremner, Robert H., et al. 1970. *Children and Youth in America: A Documentary History.* Vol. 1. Cambridge, MA: Harvard University Press.

Kappler, Charles J. 1904. *Laws and Treaties.* Vol. 1. Washington, DC: US Government Printing Office.

Unger, Steven. 1977. *The Destruction of American Indian Families.* New York: Association on American Indian Affairs.

PART 1

Truth

You can rest now, Gramma,
I am home.
Your prayers were strong, Gramma,
they guided me home.
Your blood I feel,
your blood runs strong.
It led me home.
I've heard the drum,
I've sung our songs,
Your tears have cleansed me in the sweat.
Now I'm strong.

No more hate.
No more pain.
It's never too late
to learn our ways,
to heal our hearts,
to walk in pride,
to walk in dignity,
to walk in beauty.
I have danced in the circle.
I have smoked the pipe.
I have danced and touched the Tree.
Now my heart can see
your face, Gramma,
your face in mine.
I am home.
You can rest now, Gramma.
I am home.

1

"A Child of the Indian Race"

IT WAS MARCH 1988, and I was trying to settle into my apartment. Just one month before, I had left my thirteen-year marriage and moved out with my twelve-year-old daughter and my five-year-old son. I was sick with chronic fatigue syndrome (CFS). Extreme muscle aches, fatigue, sore throat, constant earache, joint pain, and unrefreshed sleep left my mind cloudy and my spirit nearly defeated. It was impossible to work. My soon-to-be-ex-husband was furious with me and withheld child support payments. I had no money. My children were apprehensive and sad, yet I knew I was where I needed to be for my mental health and theirs.

One day, the phone rang with a call from the local rape crisis center in Madison, Wisconsin. My name had come to the top of their list for a group to address my issues and concerns. Could I come in for an assessment? I had almost forgotten that I had called them six months earlier, right after I had a strange and disconcerting blip of memory about a doctor molesting me. After hearing other women tell their stories at 12-step meetings, I had learned how important it was to heal from sexual abuse, so I had called the center. They had put my name on a waiting list, and I hung up the phone and forgot about it.

It had been eight years since I last drank. I knew from attending those 12-step meetings that in order to stay sober, I would have to address those pains that I had once drowned in alcohol. I agreed to come in for the assessment.

At my first appointment, I answered questions on a form, then sat across from the brown woman counselor. I don't recall what she said until I heard "mother-daughter incest."

I looked at her and said, "What? Are you sure?"

She said, "Sandy, what happened to you was incestuous."

I knew of male-female incest, but I'd never heard anyone talk about same-sex abuse. I was stunned—and at the same time, I felt relieved to have my secret identified. It was not something that I made up. It had a name. I was not the only one—it happened to other people. But they wanted me to participate in a ten-week group session to talk about it with other people. Now that was even scarier. But again, I was motivated to hold to my sobriety, so I agreed to attend this group.

I grew up in the country, on a farm in Wisconsin. I remember going to the top of the little hill behind the house and lying flat on my stomach, with my face nuzzled in the plush grass, and crying until I couldn't cry anymore. I wept from the outbursts of my mother's rage, the taunts from the kids at school, and that strange feeling in my body, the feeling that I instinctively knew not to talk about. I would lie there until I felt I could go back to the house without showing that I had been crying.

In joining the group, I was about to embark on a journey that would answer my childhood prayers, the prayers I said while off on my own in the fields wondering who I was.

I sat nervously on the overstuffed pillows with the other clients, seven women, all of them white. I had become so accustomed to being alone, the only brown person. I was the only Indian girl in the small town where I grew up. My adoptive mother and father were white. They were fundamentalist missionaries who adopted me from the Rosebud Sioux Reservation in South Dakota.

I kept staring at the counselors, two brown women, both Puerto Rican. I had lived in Puerto Rico for a year, while stationed at Roosevelt Roads Navy Base. I felt a kinship with these women that I didn't have words for, and I trusted them right away, which was very unusual for me.

Each week we were expected to participate in activities that would help us share. The first week, we were to make a story using all the letters of the alphabet to describe ourselves. I shocked myself by using the letter "I" to say that I was an Indian woman. I didn't usually acknowledge that reality. I was taught not to. Nobody seemed to care, anyway. But there it was on my paper, and it scared me.

While I was married to my first husband, my race was not to be discussed. He made it very clear to me that I was not to draw attention to the fact that I was Indian. I remember thinking, *how am I going to do that when I'm always asked, "What nationality are you?"* Once when we were grocery shopping, a very friendly Hispanic man was loading our groceries into our car. He said to me in Spanish, "Are you Mexican?"

I smiled and replied, "No, I am Indian."

When he left, my husband frowned and said, "You don't need to tell anyone you're Indian." I had been so acquainted with shame about my identity that I obeyed. I tried to become invisible to the world.

Then there was the group exercise that pushed me into myself. We were told to bring an object that had particular emotional significance to us. I didn't give it any thought. Just before it was time to leave for the meeting, I had no idea what to bring. I began to look for something that had "emotional significance." There were unpacked boxes all around my apartment, and I quickly ran my hands through them. *Emotional significance! I don't even know what that means!*

I fumed. I was mad at myself for putting off the assignment, and even more frustrated that I didn't have anything that had this "emotional significance."

There was one more box to go through. This box had papers: marriage certificate, discharge papers from the navy, children's birth certificates, Social Security information, . . . adoption papers.

I stopped and looked for a moment. I held the tri-folded legal document in my hand and then, without opening it, hurried to group.

As each woman described the object she brought, I began to feel guilty. They all had put so much thought into the assignment, and all I did was haphazardly grab a document that I had not even read yet! I was thirty-five years old, and I always knew I was adopted. My adoptive mom finally gave me the papers the year before, and I just never read them.

As a child, I was told repeatedly that my Indian mother drank, but I also remember being told a few facts about her. Her name was Nina. She had two children before me, Leonard and Edith. Edith's nickname was "Chop," because of the shape of her eyes and because she was really cute. I was told that Leonard lived with "an old Indian." My adoptive mom would say, "That old Indian wanted you, too, but we got you. Leonard had tuberculosis. It's a good thing we got you, because they lived out in this old shack with no running water or electricity." She said, "You just wouldn't have stood a chance there."

I don't ever remember feeling "lucky" that I wasn't back on the reservation. What I do remember is wishing I was there. I used to fantasize about what it was like. I sensed that my mom thought this "old Indian" was shameful for that way he lived. The tone of her voice and her body language always told me more than her words did. The one positive thing she told me was that my mother was pretty.

When it was my turn, I looked around at all the women. The room was already heavy with the shared emotions. I felt that I had let everyone down by not preparing for this. I apologized for my lack of participation. One of the counselors said, "What *did* you bring, Sandy?"

STATE OF SOUTH DAKOTA,
County of __Tripp.__ } ss.

IN THE MATTER OF THE ADOPTION OF)

Sandra Lee White,)

IN COUNTY COURT

ORDER DECLARING
CHILD ADOPTED

The above entitled matter having come on for hearing before the Court on this 21st day of Sept. A. D. 19 55, upon petition of _____ and _____ for an order declaring the above named Sandra Lee White to be their adopted child, the petitioners and the child appearing in Court in person and it appearing to the Court from the petition and evidence herein, and from the report of __Charles D. Dillon__, the investigator heretofore appointed by the Court, that said petitioners are husband and wife and are residents of _____, County of __Tripp__, State of South Dakota, and desire to adopt the above named child so as to make it the same as their own child, capable of inheriting their estate; that petitioners have agreed, in writing, that said child shall be treated in all respects as their own lawful child should be treated; that petitioners are each more than ten years older than said child and the child has lived within the home of petitioners for more than six months last past; that more than ten days have elapsed since the filing of said petition; that said child is a __female__ child of the __indian__ race born on __November 30th__, 19 53 at Winner, South Dakota, _____ and its full adoptive name is Sandra Lee _____: that the full names of the adopting parents are _____ a member of the __white__ race, a citizen of __the United States of America__ residing at __Tripp County, South Dakota, (P. O. Winner)__, who was born at Tripp County, South Dakota, _____ on _____ 1912, who is by occupation a __farmer__, and _____, a member of the __white__ race, a citizen of __United States of America__, residing at __Tripp County, South Dakota, (P. O. Winner)__, who was born at __Big Rock, Illinois,__ on __October__, 1910, who is by occupation a __Housewife,__

And it further appearing that said child was born out of wedlock and that her parents have not married, and that the mother, Nina Garneaux, has consented to the adoption of said child by the petitioners and by her duly executed Power of Attorney appointed Rev. Raymond Mountour as her Attorney in Fact to appear before this court and in her stead consent to the adoption of said child by the petitioners; and the petitioners Edmund Keierleber and Catherine Keierleber, the child Sandra Lee White and the Attorney in Fact, Rev. Raymond Montour, personally appearing,

And the Judge having examined separately all persons appearing, and being satisfied from such examination and report of the investigation made that the child is suitable for adoption; that the petitioners are financially able and morally fit to have the care, supervision and training of such child; that all requirements of law have been met and that the interests of said child will be promoted by the adoption,

It is hereby ORDERED, ADJUDGED and DECREED that the said __Sandra Lee White__ be the adopted child of _____ and _____ and shall be treated in all respects as the child of said petitioners; that the name of said child be changed to that of __Sandra Lee__ _____, an that petitioners pay the cost of proceeding.

Dated at __Winner,__, South Dakota, this __21st__ day of __September__ A. D. 19 55.

BY THE COURT:

J. D. Hannett
Judge of the County Court

Attest: _Alice M Hanlee_
Clerk

By _Ruth Johnson_, Deputy

The document that made my adoption final

"Just my adoption papers," I sheepishly replied.

Without missing a beat she said, "Why don't you read them?"

Now I really felt ashamed, since I didn't do the assignment as asked. Just like in school, I figured the counselor was going to embarrass me, to teach me a lesson. Out of respect to those who participated and did the work, I braced myself for the embarrassment about to be given to me. *I can take it*, I thought. I did as I was asked.

As I opened the document, I scanned it and thought, *This is like owning a pedigreed horse.* I began to read it out loud.

There were several lines with the date, the judge's name, my adoptive parents' names, my name. And then I read: "that petitioners are each more than ten years older than said child and said child has lived within the home of petitioners for more than six months last past; that more than ten days have elapsed since the filing of said petition; that said child is a female child of the *indian* race born on November 30, 1953."

I couldn't read any further. My heart was racing. My soul stung like it had been slapped. I felt ashamed—dark and ugly.

I was very young when my adoptive mother first told me who I was and where I came from. She was sitting on the edge of the bed; I was standing in front of her. Her hands held my shoulders, and she looked into my eyes as she said these words: "Your mother didn't really want you. She only wanted to keep you so she could have a welfare check so she could drink. If we hadn't gotten you, you wouldn't have had a chance. You would have had a miserable existence. You should be very grateful we took you and gave you this chance at life."

She always introduced me as her adopted Indian child. Her voice changed as she tipped her head and got a sad, distant look on her face. She sighed deeply, and then described the destitute place I was born, announcing that if she hadn't gotten me, I would never have stood a chance.

I always looked down at my shoes. My skin seemed to burn as a blanket of shame covered me from head to toe.

Posed with some of my dad's relatives in South Dakota

Each word she spoke inched that blanket over me until I was suffocating with embarrassment. And whoever she was introducing me to would look me over as if they were saying to themselves, *So this is what an Indian looks like.* She went on and on to whoever would listen, recounting the story over and over: how they were called to "work with the Indians" in South Dakota, how they came to find out about this Indian baby, and how my Indian mother drank and didn't want me. She described Indians as pagan people whose difficult lives were of their own making because they were not Christians. I felt naked, on display for study by curious adults.

Any progress I made in building my own inner sense of myself as a "normal kid" was repeatedly crushed by her introduction: "This is my adopted Indian daughter. You should see where we got her." It felt as if I were an animal she rescued. Whenever I did anything bad, it was because I was Indian. If I did anything good, it was because I was white. But how did I cross from being Indian to being white? I never could figure that out. I lived somewhere in the middle, racially blank. It was easy, since I didn't have any brown people around to compare myself with. But it was also very lonely. I thought that was where I belonged—there in that lonely dark place.

I heard this over and over again, and as time wore on, these words became my identity. I was an ungrateful, dirty, ugly little Indian kid who needed to be saved from the reservation full of people who didn't really want me, anyway. After all, I didn't even look Indian, according to my adoptive mother.

The counselor asked me what I was *feeling. Feeling?* What I was seeing in my mind were things I never told anyone. There were no *feelings,* just darkness and a strange humming numbness. I breathed hard; my head hurt; my chest felt like it was about to explode. *A child of the* Indian *race*—I don't even know what being Indian meant! I felt ashamed that I didn't know what it meant to be Indian. I was so enraged that I was reading about myself as if I were an animal! My feelings bubbled up from a dark place that I had closed the door on many years before.

One day when I was eleven, about four years after my adoptive father died, my mother had another one of her rages, in which I was the target. I just could not seem to get things right for her. I ran through the house to the top of the stairs and lay down on the floor looking over the stairwell, hiding from view. Her leg was impaired from childhood polio and she was overweight, which kept her from chasing me up the stairs.

She stood at the bottom of the stairs yelling at me. Her rage turned to frustrated crying and back to rage as she screamed, "I should have just left you on the reservation! You don't appreciate anything!"

As I lay there looking down over the landing, I shut the

door in my heart. Numbness came over me, I felt nothing, it was as if someone else was watching us and telling me what she was saying. I decided right then that she was never going to make me cry again, that no one was going to make me cry about being Indian, ever again.

Now I was thirty-five, sitting in this group, looking at the phrase, "a female child of the *indian* race." I felt the sting of those pent-up tears. I was so afraid to let them come. I gritted my teeth in anger and refused to cry. The tears pushed at my tear ducts, seeking release. The back of my throat pulled in an ache, my chest heaved as I began to breathe hard and fast. My mind raced to secure the door that was beginning to nudge open. There seemed to be a little brown girl behind the door, shyly trying to peek out. I didn't know what was happening to me. I began thinking that maybe I was going crazy and hallucinating!

The counselor gently asked me again to say what I was *feeling*. I thought I *was* talking! I looked up and said, "It says 'child of the *Indian* race,' and I don't know what that means!" Yet I did know what it meant. It meant ugliness, shame, and hatred. I felt ashamed because I didn't know what it meant to be Indian. But I felt even more shame because I was secretly *proud* of being Indian. How could I be *proud* when I didn't know what it meant?

Finally, out of fatigue, I opened that wound in my heart and began to let the tears come. I wept deeply. I cried like a little girl. My mind kept trying to stop me. *Don't go too far, Sandy, you might not come back. That was a long time ago. Don't let them see this. You may not make it back from this black hole of pain and confusion.*

But I was tired and my heart was so weary. I cried, I swore, I yelled. It felt like I was puking up years of sickness. Then, to my surprise, the women in the group showed compassion for me. They told me that they could *understand* how confusing and hurtful this was for me. *Understand?* No one had ever understood. I didn't know how to receive this expression of compassion. It felt so foreign and uncomfortable. I was more acquainted with shame and disapproval than kindness and compassion. I reluctantly let some of the kindness in, mostly pretending like I was receiving it. I didn't know what else to do.

I sat nervously on the overstuffed pillows, now a little brown girl in a grown-up body. A little brown girl who was once a little brown baby transported from the arms of her brown family to the arms of this white missionary family. I remembered that day.

I used to think I made this up. But I asked my adoptive mother if this had happened, and she confirmed it was true.

She told me that I was placed with a white woman from the church until they got custody of me. I remember being lifted and passed into a red pickup and placed between two unfamiliar people. I remember how the pedals looked on the floor of the old pickup, the starter button sticking out of the floor next to the accelerator, the clutch and brake and the long skinny black stick shift with a ball on the top and the sour smell of the white arm trying to hold me. The next memory is of me hiding under a table. Actually, what I remember is seeing a little brown girl hiding under a table and a woman trying to coax her out. That little brown girl was me. The table was my new adoptive parents' kitchen table.

I was hiding under there because I was scared! They weren't my parents. Nothing was familiar. I was eighteen months old. I knew who my family was. I had a sense of "home," and this was not it. It must have been so frightening to me that I left my body, which

Me at eighteen months. Look closely at my eyes. I am sad, mad, and terrified, all at once.

TRUTH

is why it seems like I was watching this. My adoptive mother always told me that I hid from her because I was so hurt by my Indian family. "You were a nervous wreck when we got you. It was just horrible." Then she would shake her head in disgust and tell me some ugly story of a drunken Indian and how lucky I was to be adopted and saved from that destitute life. God damn it! I hid because I was scared of *her!* She was not my mother. This was not my home. Nothing smelled or looked like home. I was eighteen months old. I was already bonded to a family. Whether or not they were poor, whether or not they were drinking, I instinctively knew who my family was and what it felt like to be with them. My adoptive mom would not have told it that way. I hated her even more. I hid under that table and cried because I missed my mother and family. What was I going to do with all this rage and hurt?

The weeks passed. I sat on those overstuffed pillows in the room with white women, now as "an adult of the *Indian* race," alone again but strangely hopeful. We did visualization exercises. We brought childhood pictures and talked about what was going on at the times the pictures were taken. As we all listened to each other, we nurtured each other and began to learn to nurture ourselves. Together we began our individual journeys of healing. I am eternally grateful for this experience, as it is what gave me the courage to take the next step.

At the end of the ten-week session, I had a one-on-one with my counselor. She talked about the work I did in group, and together we talked about my further healing. Then she said, "Sandy, as a counselor, I cannot tell you what to do. I can only suggest and give you feedback. But I am going to tell you this. You do not know what it is to be a woman of color, and that is what you are. You were culturally raped by being taken away. All the things that have happened to you since then stem from that, from being taken away. I don't know how you are going to do it, but you need to find out how to be that woman of color you are."

I left the office with the words "culturally raped" ringing

in my ears. I wanted to believe it. Hearing that made me feel somewhat relieved—but at the same time, I wanted to minimize that statement. After that last appointment, I went home and opened the box that held my "item of emotional significance," found the probate papers sent to me by the tribe when my Indian mother died, found the list of siblings, and wrote a letter to my oldest sister, Edith. I introduced myself, told her what I knew about her from stories my adoptive mother had told me. I told her that I would like to meet her.

I had spent so long hiding out emotionally that I could only entertain the idea of finding out who I was for small bits of time. I sent the letter, then quit thinking about it.

And then, three months later, my friend Cindy told me she was going to Colorado for a weeklong training. She could take a spouse, but since she didn't have a spouse, did I want to go? I said, "Sure. Can we go via South Dakota, so I can stop at the reservation and meet my family?"

And that's what we did.

2

The First Trip Home

CINDY AND I STARTED from Madison, Wisconsin, and made it as far as Murdo, South Dakota, about fifty miles from Rosebud, where we spent the night. We awoke to a warm, sunny Saturday in July. After breakfast, we headed south across I-90 to Highway 83, a straight shot to the reservation. We had allowed a full day for this side trip.

As we drove into the countryside, I was so very aware that I had been in the city for way too long. I grew up in the country and loved the quiet, the smells, and the beauty of the land. But this countryside had very few trees. The plains seemed to go on forever, and I suddenly realized that this made me uneasy. I had to become comfortable with the fact that I was insignificant to the horizon, yet I was wholly part of it at the same time.

After about forty-five minutes, we hit the intersection to turn on Highway 18 to go to Rosebud. We turned right, and then left, and then I saw it: a sign saying "The Land of the Burnt Thigh." I had no idea what that meant. I stared as long as I could in the passing car, saying it over in my head, *Land of the Burnt Thigh.*

I scanned the landscape. I couldn't explain it and didn't

really want to say anything, but it was as if I could feel fresh air in my nostrils, as if I just stepped out of an overly dusty room. That is ironic, since there was dust in the air. There always is, in South Dakota. But that's how it felt, like my lungs were breathing fresh air for the first time. I felt like something opened. And I had not even spoken to anyone yet.

We drove into Rosebud. I looked around as the people were going about their daily routines. We pulled into the parking lot at the tribal courthouse. I walked in with my probate envelope in hand and asked the woman behind the desk, "Do you know Edith White Hawk? Or Leonard Medicine Eagle?" She shook her head and tried not to engage me too much. She suggested I go to the post office next door. I walked over, asked the same question, and got the same response. I walked back to the car and told Cindy, "Let's drive around."

We drove up into the housing area right next to the tribal courthouse. I could see the different houses—flowers or toys in some yards, broken-down cars in others, kids playing in the street, dogs crossing lazily from one side of the road to the other. I was taking it all in, thinking, *This is where I would have grown up, maybe even lived in this house right here.* And also, *One of these guys might be my relative.*

As we drove out of the housing area, we saw a man walking on the road. I told my friend, "Stop. Let's ask him." The car stopped. I introduced myself and said I was looking for my sister Edith or my brother Leonard. He told me to try talking with someone at the senior housing. It was nearby, so we drove to the long building that reminded me of a motel.

Outside one of the doors sat a white-haired, round gramma wearing those old brown polyester pants with the seam down the front, a flowered cotton smock top with wide pockets on each side, and gray gramma shoes. She was enjoying the cool morning air in the shade, sipping coffee, smoking a cigarette. I got out of the car and went up to her and once again said, "My name is Sandy Reynolds." That was my married name. "I'm from here, but I was adopted. I'm looking for my sister Edith and my brother Leonard."

She asked me, "Do you know who your mother is?"

"Nina Lulu White Hawk Garneaux," I replied. That was how the name was written on the papers I carried.

"I knew your mother," she replied. When I asked her for more information, she suggested that I go to the hospital and see if anyone up there would help me. I thanked her, returned to the car, and gave my friend the directions to the hospital.

As we drove up a small hill and then rounded down to the hospital, I was taken by surprise. I remembered being here before.

I was about four years old, riding in the back seat of our family car. We drove slowly up this hill and then down the other side and turned into a driveway. I had looked into the rearview mirror and saw the collar of my dress. It was one of my church dresses. I felt good in it, and I was admiring the little white scalloped collar. Then I looked up and saw this red brick building and a nurse dressed in her uniform carrying a small bundle to our car. My adoptive mother was with her. The nurse put the bundle next to me in the back seat. The bundle was my new baby brother. I got excited as I looked at him swaddled and asleep in the back seat. I stared at him, and I could hear the gravel under the tires, and then I remember trying to pry his eyes open. I must have thought his eyes would work like doll eyes that closed when you lay them down. As I tried to pry them open, he began to cry, and I got a spanking.

It was Saturday, and the side entrance seemed the only way to enter. We walked into the small hospital lobby. I have always read what is on bulletin boards, so I began to peruse the one I saw there. I spotted an announcement for a Sundance, a rectangle poster that had Lakota written on one side. The other side, in English, said, "Come and pray with us so that all our children will be returned to us." I felt like I was going to cry. I wanted to run to tell someone, "Hey, this is me; I am one of those you prayed home." But I kept quiet.

Then an Indian man about my age walked into the lobby

from a hallway in the back. He had a long ponytail and a welcoming smile. He greeted me and asked if I was looking for someone and could he help. I repeated my introduction to him, resisting the urge to say, "I am one of the ones that has been prayed home," and stuck to the boring details.

I told him I was looking for Edith and Leonard, and he said that he had known Leonard since he was young. I was so excited to hear that, I said, "Do I look like him?"

He scanned my face and said, "Yes, you have the same smile." His name was Chuck Holquin. He explained that he was a mental health worker and had stopped in on his day off to help a young woman. He invited us into his office.

After a few words, he said, "I can take you around the reservation and see if we can find anyone who knew your mother." I jumped at the offer, but Cindy looked scared. I took her to the side, and when I asked her what was wrong, it became apparent that she was uncomfortable being the only white person around. Then I realized how comfortable I felt. Wow, the tables were finally turned! I was not alone. I was not the only Indian.

Cindy and I agreed that I would sit next to the stranger in his truck. We drove the few miles to St. Francis and went into a few homes. At some of them, Chuck spoke Lakota, and we waited for the English translation. No one we talked with seemed to know my mother, Nina. In the truck on the way back to Chuck's office, I began telling him that I was sad that I finally made it to the reservation only after my mother had passed on.

He told me, "Your mother has always been here waiting for you. Here she is"—and he stretched out his arm with the palm of his hand up, indicating the landscape. "This land is your mother. She was always here and she welcomes you home." I couldn't say anything. I somehow understood in my heart, remembering how I lay on the ground at the top of the hill behind my house, snuggled in the plush grass as if I was crying on someone's shoulder.

Me and Chuck Holquin, who found my family

When we got back to his office, Chuck got on the phone right away, asking different people about Nina Lulu White Hawk Garneaux. Finally, I heard him say, "Oh, okay, yes," and he wrote down some names. He hung up and handed me the paper, telling me, "These are your uncles—Torrence Fast Horse, Manfred Fast Horse, and Clifford Fast Horse. They're in O'Kreek right now at a softball game. I'll go over there with you, if you want."

As we walked to the car, he explained that my mother was born before my grandmother married Paul Fast Horse, so all my aunts and uncles were Fast Horses. This time we got in Cindy's car. She was happy to be back in the driver's seat.

O'Kreek was about thirty miles from Rosebud. We drove

down to the ball field and parked the car. I got out, holding a large brown envelope.

Nina Garneaux died in 1984. Sometime in 1986, I received the probate material in a large brown envelope. I had tucked it away because I was numb yet to my connection to my birth mother and tribe. I tucked it away where I tucked the shame, hurt, and anger, and I didn't think about it again, until now. Even while I was carrying it with me in South Dakota, there was not any emotion connected to it. I took it everywhere. I guess it was my proof of who I was, just in case someone didn't believe me.

That paper is the outside of who I am, but I don't need a paper to show who I am. That comes from within. I was still disconnected from myself. This piece of paper said I was from here, this land, this place; I was from an Indian mother from Rosebud. Another piece of paper—my adoption decree— said I was no longer living with my Indian mother and that I belonged to my adoptive parents. I stood somewhere in the middle of these realities. I was Outside Inside the Self.

As he got out of the car, Chuck said, "There's your uncles over there." He motioned to a concession stand. We walked over, and Chuck approached one of the men. They spoke in Indian for a while, then I heard, "Sandy, Nina's daughter," as he stepped aside for me to step forward.

My uncle Clifford looked at me and smiled big and said, "Sure you are. I always wondered how you were doing out East."

I was momentarily at a loss for words, but I started talking nonstop. Chuck later suggested I try to not be so forward. But I wasn't quite sure what that meant, and I was too excited to ask. Adoptees commonly feel the loss of how to be a member of their birth cultures. How to act, when to talk, when not to ask questions, how to go with the flow, how to trust that in time everything unfolds to the good. It was my first lesson in the very different communication styles of Lakota people, and that I only knew how to communicate in the way I was raised—white.

But they were patient with me. My uncle Terry came over, introduced himself, and told me that the softball game was a tournament for a relative of ours who had died in a car accident. He said, "You're related to everyone here." I looked around and saw at least seventy-five people. I couldn't comprehend that. My adoptive mother was an only child, and we didn't see my adoptive father's family, back in South Dakota. I didn't grow up with cousins, aunts, uncles, or grandparents.

As we were visiting, a car parked in the space next to my uncle's van. A woman got out and came over to talk to one of my uncles. Then she said, "You must be Deborah."

With Uncle Clifford, Aunt Cecilia, and Uncle Terry, on that first trip to Rosebud. I'm in shorts.

I said, "No, I'm Sandy."

Then she said, "Oh, you're the one who wrote Edith. I got the letter. Edith doesn't live here. I'm your auntie Cecilia."

She then began to fill me in on some family history and said, "You need to come meet Uncle Manfred." Cindy was okay hanging out at the tournament, so I excitedly hopped into Aunt Cecilia's car. She was moving, and she just happened to have boxes of pictures in the back seat. She gave me a picture of Edith. We drove to a house not far away where a man was fixing a car in the driveway. She said to the man, "This is Nina's daughter." And then she turned to me and said, "This is your uncle John." We shared a few questions. He smiled, said he remembered me and was glad I made it back.

Then we went to meet Uncle Manfred. Cecilia said that he was the patriarch of the family. Since my mother had passed, he was now the oldest. She told me my mother was the oldest of twenty children. We entered his home and Cecilia introduced me. I will always remember his smile and his eyes as they took in my face. Was he looking for resemblances to his sister? I was looking into his face for any resemblance of me. He told me a few things about my mother and where we lived when I was a baby. Then he told me to make sure I came back, that this was my home. I left feeling so good and happy but also not quite sure how to act. I had never been a niece before, and I didn't know what that kind of relationship meant. I especially didn't know what it meant in the Lakota way.

As I met family members, they often would simply say, "Oh yeah, I remember you" and then tell their story. They remembered me because I wasn't taken away until I was eighteen months old. Before I was taken, apparently, I had lived in different family members' homes. One uncle teased me because he always got stuck babysitting me along with other young family members. Now that I was back, it felt good to be a part of a family again.

They told me of other relatives who had been in foster care or adopted out. They talked about boarding schools and how that had affected our family. I learned more about adoptions in the 1950s and 1960s, when infertile white couples were desperate to adopt during the baby boom, and many, many Indian families lost their children. I began to see how I fit in to this history.

We went on to Cindy's conference in Colorado Springs, where I attended a few sessions and tried to get used to the idea of having a family at Rosebud. When it was over, we got up early to start the eight-hour trip back to Winner, South Dakota, a town about seventeen miles east of the Rosebud Reservation. I was excited to look for my brother. Chuck Holquin had drawn a map of the housing development in Winner where Leonard lived.

It was a beautiful day to be on the road. The sun shone brightly, drawing up dancing heat waves from the pavement. On one long, flat stretch, we saw a herd of elk running in the field next to the highway.

We finally pulled into Winner late in the day. The weariness of the long trip seemed to fall away as we found the Indian housing. I used the map to guide Cindy onto the right street. We drove into the driveway of my brother's house. No one was home. A man and a child sat on the front stoop of the house next door. I left Cindy in the car and walked over to him, introducing myself as Leonard Medicine Eagle's sister. "Does he live here?" I pointed to the house.

"Yes, he does, but they're gone right now," the neighbor replied. "Have a seat." He pointed to a kitchen chair that was now serving as a patio chair. "So, you're his sister?"

"Yes, I am. I was adopted out when I was eighteen months old and raised in Wisconsin," I said and stopped.

We sat in silence awhile. He sipped a beer as Hank Williams's "There's a Tear in My Beer" played from a boom box sitting in a window. We made some more small talk, and then he said, "There's Leonard's wife now."

A brown car carrying a woman and a couple of children pulled into their driveway. I thanked the neighbor for his hospitality and walked over to Leonard's wife. "Hi, I'm Sandy," I said. "I'm Leonard's sister."

As we shook hands, she said, "My name is Sandra, Leonard's wife. We heard about you." She smiled an excited smile and said, "Leonard is painting a house in town. We can go over there. He'll be glad to see you." Cindy and I followed Sandra's car to the house Leonard was painting, three minutes away. Leonard was on a ladder with a paintbrush in his hand. He looked over when he saw us all getting out of our cars. "Leonard, someone wants to meet you. Your sister."

I started toward him as he stepped down from the ladder. We walked toward each other smiling. We embraced as he said, "Hi, Sister," and I said, "I love your smile." Sandra and Cindy watched our reunion with big smiles on their faces.

It is a strange feeling to sense a connection that you have no words for and didn't create through shared experiences. It was just there; it has to be DNA. We carry the same blood; we grew in the same womb. We spent a lot of time just looking at each other and smiling. Seeing Leonard was like seeing my face for the first time. My brother and his wife and their three children—Chris, Leon, and Alicia—gave me the sense of family and reconnection to the land where I took my first steps as a toddler.

It was time to go back to Wisconsin, and we took one more ride around the small town of Winner.

We drove down Main Street, and I saw my uncle Manfred standing on a street corner in front of the Pamida store. We waved and smiled at each other. After we passed, I watched him through the back window. He stood and watched the car awhile before he crossed the street. I wondered what he was thinking. Was he talking to his sister, telling her I was home? Was he thanking the Creator for my return?

Then it hit me. When I was adopted, we had lived near Winner. The words of my adoptive mother came back to me: "We moved to Wisconsin so you'd have a better chance." Some better chance. I hit the dashboard with my fist and

The day we met: with my brother Leonard, his wife Sandra, and their children Alicia and Leon. Their son Chris is not in the picture.

yelled, "She didn't move so I'd have a better chance! She moved because with nineteen aunts and uncles and all their children, my cousins, I was bound to always see a relative!"

It would constantly remind her that I had a family. And wouldn't I recognize my mother or other relatives if we passed each other on the streets of Winner? How would she handle it when a relative saw her with me? They all knew who adopted me. If they saw her on the street and waved, would she wave back? Would she warn me not to talk to the pagan Indians, because they didn't love Jesus? My adoptive mother was insecure and unstable. Always running into my relatives would have been too much for her. Besides, South Dakota was not her homeland. She was from Illinois.

* * *

So there it was. My first trip home to Rosebud opened the door to healing the pain of separation from my identity. I remembered the abuse, began to talk about the confusing times. I had learned in group how to nurture myself when the memories came. I also had the fellowship of those in 12-step meetings. I had friends who would listen to me process, over and over again, as I began to put my life in perspective, trying to figure out why and how the Creator could have let all this unfold.

When I looked again at my adoption papers, I found the evaluation by Charles P. Dillon, the social worker. He noted the "handicaps for Sandra in this placement," including my birth mother's knowing where I was and my adoptive parents' lack of flexibility. "Normal teenage problems could lead to complications and rejection of the child. The strictness of the [adoptive parents] is in the area of religion which will not permit a child to have normal entertainment such as shows and other entertainment." Still, he made a "favorable recommendation . . . with oral reservations."

I became so enraged it scared me. But I pressed on to reveal those pictures in my head that I now realize were memories. In order to protect me, my mind had categorized them as "blips" of something other than memories of my young life. Like putting them in a drawer until the time was right. The time had arrived and the memories flowed like raging water, suddenly released from behind a dam.

Adoption of: Sandra Lee White

By: Mr. and Mrs. ████ ████

Placement: Sandra Lee White was placed in the ████ home in March of 1955 by the child's mother, Nina Garneaux.

Home: Mr. and Mrs. ████ live in a four-room fram dwelling on a farm ten miles west and ten miles south of Winner, South Dakota. The home is adequate for space.

Adoptive Parents: ████ ████ was born April 24, 1912, in Tripp County, South Dakota, of German parentage. Mr. ████ had an eighth grade education and is employed as a farmer. He is now farming 100 acres and has four quarters of hayland under lease. He has 75 head of cattle including calves and the annual income was given as $5000.

Mrs. ████ was born October 10, 1909, in Illinois. Her maiden name was ████
Mrs. ████ completed high school and has had some college education.in music.
Mrs. ████'s work experience, other than music, was work in a mental hospital for 14 months. Her nationality background is Welch, Swiss and Luxenborg German.

Child: Sandra Lee White was born November 30, 1953, at Winner, South Dakota, of French and Indian background on the mother's side and an unknown parentage on the father's side. Sandra Lee was seen as an active normal child of average intelligence. Her health and development has been good.

Natural Mother: Nina Lula Garneaux was born January 3, 1933, at the Rosebud Hospital of French and Indian parentage. Nina completed the ninth grade and quit because of rebellion. Her grades in school were average. Nina has had no work experience and is an unstable person.

Natural Father: Sandra's father is in his 20's and is employed as a salesman. His nationality is not known.

Evaluation: There are handicaps for Sandra in this placement. The mother's knowledge of the whereabouts of the child can lead to interference and unhappiness for her. The ████ were not seen as very flexible people and normal teenage problems could lead to complications and rejection of the child. The strictness of the ████ is in the area of religion which will not permit a child to have normal entertainment such as shows and other entertainment.

Recommendation: A favorable recommendation of the adoption of Sandra Lee White by Mr. and Mrs. ████ ████ has been given with oral reservations.

Charles P. Dillon
Child Welfare Worker

September 15, 1955

A photocopy of Charles P. Dillon's Report to the Court, recommending my adoption

3

Growing Up, Growing Alone

I WAS FOUR WHEN WE MOVED from the house in South Dakota, but I can still see the kitchen, where the sink was, where the kitchen table was, the living room, and the bedroom. How are these memories with me after all these years—the sights, sounds, and smells, the energy in each room?

My adoptive parents lived and worked a small ranch with beef cattle, about twenty miles from the town of Winner. My dad took me with him as he surveyed the cattle out on the range. I loved the excitement of riding in the Jeep, hanging on as we drove over bumps and through the shallow parts of creeks. My mom told me that I could tell if a cow was ready to deliver her calf. I felt joy with my adoptive father. He was a tall, thick man with large hands and a shy smile. He always wore blue, bibbed overalls with a blue work shirt.

One day the Jeep must have broken down, because we walked home from the field. My adoptive father lifted me to his shoulders and I could see so much from there. His strides were long and strong, crunching rhythmically and kicking up gravel with each step. I rode in complete comfort, my legs rubbing against the buckles on his bib overalls and my feet tucked under his arms. The sun was warm, the grasshoppers were hopping alongside the road, and the magpies sang a song just for us. I felt happy.

I trusted my adoptive dad.

Then the good feelings stop abruptly, as they did regularly in my life. My adoptive mother sat in the chair, holding me tightly as I struggled to get loose from her grip. We were both naked. Her breathing was a shallow pant that made my body weak with what I came to recognize as shame. I was held close enough to stare into the large pores on her skin, and I was overcome by that sour smell that I first smelled in the red truck. Once again, I left my body and became someone watching the small brown baby struggle against the arms of the mother that scared her so. She sat there with me naked and rocked in the chair, staring at me with a look of excited desperation.

Just then the door opened, and the sun behind my dad's large frame shadowed his face from me. My mother startled, jumped up, put me on the floor, and ran to the bedroom. I don't remember being comforted by him or anything after that.

I will spare you the ugly details of the many memories of these times with my mother. I understood nothing. All I knew then was how sick in my body I felt when she touched me.

So it went in my life in South Dakota. Times with my father were adventures full of the land's sights and sounds and all it offered. Times with my mother were secretive, terrifying. As I grew older, I found ways to avoid being physically close to her.

My father had horses, and I got to ride them. I remember the smell of the leather saddle and the squeak it made when my body weight shifted. Once I slipped and fell off, and I lay under the horse looking up at his belly. My dad lifted me up and placed me right back in the saddle.

My dad took me to the sale barn, which was full smells— cattle, manure, grain—and the auctioneer's chant. We sat on the bleachers watching as cattle were paraded around the center of the barn for all to observe and make their bids. I was with my dad, and all was well again.

Once he purchased a Scottish Highlander bull with very

Thanks to my dad, I got used to horses early.

large horns. We transported him home in the red truck. The great bull thrust his body against the truck walls, and the truck shifted with his massive strength. He wailed with all his might, contesting the restraints of the truck bed. My heart pounded with excitement.

My mom used to tell the story of how his horns measured thirty-two inches from the tip of one horn to the tip of the other. He lost his magnificent horns one day. I hung onto the fence, watching him fight against the men who shaved them off.

I don't remember the big sale before we moved to Wisconsin. I do remember waking up in a makeshift bed in the back seat of the Studebaker. The sun was shining, and we had just pulled off the road. I sensed excitement, but I had no idea what was going on and went back to sleep.

We had moved to a farm outside of Cazenovia, Wisconsin, about thirty miles west of Wisconsin Dells. Every few years I drive there to bring back the good memories I had there. The good memories before my father died.

The farm was tucked away in a wooded rural area about ninety miles northwest of Madison. It is beautiful country. The green is so green you can smell it. The house stood at the top of a quarter-mile-long gravel driveway. I loved to make the trek to the mailbox, which was on the main road. One day a garter snake scurried between my legs. I wasn't scared, just in awe of how he seemed to appear, slithering on his way as if he had a destination.

A creek ran under a small wooden bridge, and it held many adventures for me. I loved how the bridge rattled when we drove or walked over it. I played on the banks of that creek for hours, lost in my imagination. I saw a lone crane and gasped; since I didn't know what I was seeing, to me it was sacred. I found crawfish under the rocks, played with toads, watched and listened to the pounding of a woodpecker, the buzz of the grasshoppers. The whippoorwill's call reminded me that it was time to head home. The peaceful songs of the meadow creatures settled my spirit.

The house had a wraparound, screened-in porch that provided shelter from the mosquitoes. Just inside the back door (which seemed like the front door because it was the door we always used) was the mudroom with a sink. One day my dad held his hand under the running water as the sink filled up with blood. He had hurt his hand in the corn picker, and we had to rush to the hospital. The kitchen was huge, with a pantry. There were two rooms off the kitchen—the dining room and, on the other side, the playroom for my brother and me. My prize possession was the large blackboard and chalk. The dining room was divided from the living room by glass French pocket doors. I loved pulling those doors out and creating my private living room. The hardwood floors throughout the

My brother and I shared the sandbox.

house provided a great skating rink. There were three bed-rooms and one bathroom upstairs.

The yard was huge. Under a large oak tree sat our swing set and tractor-tire sandbox. The sandbox was my favor-ite, because I could create my own farm fields with our toy tractors and plows. I was a tomboy, always having more fun with boy toys than girl toys. One Christmas I got a double-holster six-shooter gun set, just like the one Matt Dillon car-ried on *Gunsmoke*. The belt had slots with silver bullets that fit perfectly in the guns. I was in my glory as I practiced quick-drawing my guns and saying with the toughest squint I could muster, "Get outta Dodge."

Halfway between the house and barn was my dad's tool-shed. This shed was another playground full of the smell of rust and metal. He showed me that if we poured Coca Cola over rusty bolts, the rust came off! There is a kind of mucky, gooey black dirt that collects on metal. I loved to scrape it off while my dad welded.

Next to the toolshed was the garden. We had blackberry and raspberry bushes and strawberries, beans, beets, turnips, and potatoes. My mom spent a lot of time tending to the garden. I was glad not to have to help her. I was my dad's helper. His work seemed so much more interesting. I thought riding on the tractor with my dad watching the manure spreader was a great way to spend the day. He carried an old soup can on the tractor, and when we needed a break and were thirsty, we used that can to take ice-cold water from the spring-fed creek. He showed me the mint plants. We picked them, held them to our noses, and sat in peaceful, nurturing silence.

Once, my dad woke me up and we crept down to the basement to see a bantam hen in the coal bin with her nest of eggs. They were beginning to hatch, and my dad wanted me to see this miracle. We sat together quietly and watched as an egg slowly cracked. I could hear muffled peeping from within the egg. I studied the hen's beautiful feathers to help resist the urge to pick up the egg and help the chick out. The mother hen sat nervously watching our hands, waiting to strike if we got too close. I don't remember the sound of my father's voice. I do remember the sound of the silence we shared.

These were the days before parents were warned about the limitations of children helping with chores. My dad would set me on the small Alice Chalmers tractor, tell me to hold the steering wheel straight, and away I'd go. He'd put the tractor in low gear and work behind it on foot as we laid wire for a fence. It went pretty well until one day I hit a rut that took the front tire up on a hill and nearly tipped me over. I looked back, feeling helpless, as my five-year-old arms were not strong enough to pull the tractor out of it. My dad ran to the tractor and jumped on just in time to keep it

I loved sitting in the Jeep.

My brother and I stand in front of Red Oak School, August 1960.

from tipping. After he got us back on track, we went right back to work. We later told my mother, and she gasped and asked him not to take me anymore. He looked at me and winked. I knew I was not in any danger of losing my position as his field hand.

When it was time for me to start school, I was very excited. The one-room schoolhouse was not far from where we lived. Each grade had its own row. When it was our turn for a lesson, the teacher had us come to the front of the room and sit in a circle. I loved reading and couldn't wait until the next phonics lesson. One student couldn't read very well, and he was hardly ever rewarded, as we were, with Lifesavers candy. He was even spanked, and I felt so bad for him.

We listened to the radio for music class, singing along to "The Streets of Laredo" and other cowboy songs that made me cry. There was no indoor plumbing, so we used an outhouse and brought water in from the pump. Yes, there was always someone being tricked into placing his or her tongue on the pump handle in the bitter cold winter! I loved the daily routine of taking goiter pills at milk break. The milk was a treat that we tried to make last as long as possible. It came in miniature thick glass milk bottles, and we drank through paper straws. I was taught to tie my shoes by an older girl as we sat in the shade during recess. She was so proud to have taught me and I was proud to have learned, and together we showed off to the others. School was easy and fun.

We didn't get company very often, but one year a family paid us a visit. Raymond and Francis Montour and their daughters were an Indian family from the Rosebud Reservation. I had fun playing with the girls. We played, laughed, and slept together. I remember their brown skin and deep black hair. I later found out that this family was one of the families that was instrumental in my mom and dad adopting me.

Raymond was the pastor of the church in Winner that my parents attended. He had power of attorney for my mother,

Nina, in my adoption. I don't harbor any ill will against this family. They were doing what they thought was the best thing for me. I believe that if they knew how I would suffer, and how alienated I felt, they would not have recommended I be adopted out. Who would?

I had an odd memory. I am standing in the kitchen, and I see a little brown girl standing on a chair in the mudroom, at least twenty feet away, looking in the mirror. I can still see her chest heaving as she tries to pull her short hair down to reach her shoulders. I can see her whimpering, and how she tries to hide as I approach her and gently look over her shoulders. Her brown eyes are red from crying. I can even feel the sting of shame she is feeling. *Does this mean I'm a boy now?* Why does she feel so odd, awkward, and alone?

Years later, I remembered that I was the one who was looking in the mirror crying. It was the first time my mom made me get my long, thick, wavy hair cut short and permed. I felt so ugly. My adoptive mother's voice rang in my ears as she tried to comb out the tightly permed curls, saying, "Your hair was too long and straggly." Straggly or not, it was mine, and I wanted it back.

Each season on the farm was beautiful, and each had an effect on travel. In the winter, the buildings, fences, and trees were covered in a blanket of snow, and we had to go slow. In the spring we had to go a little faster through the muddy parts, so we wouldn't get stuck. The summer and fall allowed us free sailing through the stuffy gravel dust.

We attended a small church in a little town about fifteen miles away. I stood in front of the congregation in my orange polka dot dress. I looked at my dad. He smiled his shy smile, and I began, "Genesis, Exodus, Leviticus, Deuteronomy," all the way to "Revelation." I had memorized all sixty-six books of the Bible. My mother was so proud of me. This accomplishment was huge for her. "You knew all sixty-six books of the Bible when you were five." I'm not sure what that meant to her, or what it was supposed to mean to me. Perhaps she saw it as some spiritual assurance that I wouldn't be a heathen. I don't remember her ever saying, "You had a good memory from an early age."

On Sundays after church, we had a big breakfast. Bacon, eggs, fried potatoes, and pancakes cooked in a cast iron skillet. The last pancake was always for the dog. He got a pan-sized pancake. It seemed everybody was happy on Sunday. My dad and I took the peelings from baked potatoes that had a little "meat" on them, buttered them, and put them under the broiler. We sat together at the table, anticipating our treat.

One quiet winter night I woke up on the sled being pulled by my dad as he and my mom walked to the house after the evening chores. The stars shone bright. As I lay there basking in the awe of the night sky, I could see my breath in the moonlight. The crunch of the snow from their footsteps along with the sound of the sled runners in the snow was the only noise as they walked in silence. I felt safe and secure.

There were endless ways to entertain myself while my mom and dad milked the cows and did the chores. I loved playing with the baby calves. I used to let them suck my hands. Their coarse tongues tickled. I could pull my hand away, spread my fingers, and watch the designs that appeared in the web of saliva. My days were full of the joys of the animals, and the land provided a never-ending playground full of surprises and yet always remaining constant. I was happy. Then my life again abruptly changed.

My brother and I had just gotten up and sat at the top of the stairs in our pajamas, giggling together. "When is Daddy coming home?" I asked. My mother stood at the bottom of the stairs looking up at us. Her face was red, her eyes dark with sadness, and her voice cracked as she strained to get the words out. She looked away and said, "Your daddy is never coming home again." I don't remember if she explained that he died or not. My body felt heavy and afraid and I was sad.

My adoptive dad died in a farming accident when I was six

years old. It was a confusing time. Our house was suddenly full of people. The only relatives I ever knew of, my mother's cousins Bessie and Russell, were there. I was hot and sick. My brother and I had contracted the measles. Cousin Bessie, already an elder, brought me a book, *Jack and the Beanstalk*. It was the most beautiful book I had ever seen. The pictures were vivid on the thick, glossy pages. I read and reread that book, always finding something in the pictures I missed before. At the wake, I stood next to the coffin. I didn't understand why my daddy was sleeping in that pretty box. I reached over to touch him and heard gasps from adults around me, which made me jerk my hand back. I took my last look and walked to the chairs. The next thing I remember was riding in the car as my mother drove us up to the little church in Valton, where he was buried. She was wearing a black dress and a black hat with black netting over her eyes. She was crying, and I asked her, "Why are you crying, Mom?"

She said, "Because I will never see your daddy here on earth again." In my small way I understood that I, too, would never see him again.

I had only a few years with my adoptive dad. He taught me to get back up after falling. He taught me that sitting in silence is true spiritual intimacy. Because of him, I know that men can be gentle and kind. The silence we shared was pure love and acceptance.

My mother was left to run the farm herself. She must have been so afraid and unsure. We had a hired hand, but a hired hand's heart isn't in the lifeblood of the farm. He works for his pay, not for the land. She lost the farm, and we moved into a rented house in Cazenovia. She took a job as a nursing assistant in a nursing home in Hillsboro, about seventeen miles away. She worked the night shift, 11:00 PM to 7:00 AM. I was seven and my brother was four. She put us to bed and drove off to her job, leaving us alone in the house. When a neighbor found out, they had their oldest daughter come and stay with us.

About three years later, we moved from Cazenovia to Reedsburg, a small town fifteen miles from Cazenovia. My mother bought a house one mile from town and three miles from her job at another nursing home. Once again, she left us alone while she went to work the night shift, 11:00 PM to 7:00 AM. I was afraid, but I didn't ever tell her or anyone else about it. I would wake up when she left, and then I would get dressed for school, turn on all the lights, and try to fall back asleep. When her employer found out that she was leaving us alone at night, they told her that if she did not get a babysitter or take the day shift, she would be fired. So she began working the day shift. It was much easier to be alone a short time in the morning. But all of this showed me that I was on my own.

It was difficult to start over in a new school. I was in the fifth grade, and I missed my friends from Cazenovia. I had never ridden a school bus, and it was scary to ride alone. I seemed to be sick all the time—I kept getting strep throat. My absences were suspect, and the teachers talked about me in hushed voices in my presence. Adults forget how perceptive young people are.

I was standing in the lunch line. As usual, I stood gazing into the glass display case, looking at the 4-H and sports trophies. I was glad they were there for me to stare at every day, since I did not really talk with anyone. It seemed everyone had friends, and I was not included. Shy by nature, I was not going to push myself onto anyone.

Suddenly my chest was gripped with pain. I curled my shoulders, hands to heart, short of breath, feeling dizzy and weak. I could not stand up. I began to cry with pain and fear. The other kids were looking at me—whispering, some sneering, taunting the new kid in school. A teacher came over and asked me what was wrong. I could not explain other than my chest hurt so badly. The teacher took me to a cot to lie down. Some other teachers came and looked in on me. No one extended a kind pat on the head or a reassuring stroke on my hand, telling me that I would be okay. They stood around me and whispered. "She's that adopted Indian girl. Her mom works at the nursing home." And then they all shook their heads, leaving me to see and understand that I was not like them or the other children, not to be touched—to be kept at a distance.

One teacher came in, looked at me, and then said, "She's faking."

My mother finally arrived and took me to the doctor. My heart was racing, one hundred and fifty-six beats per minute. I was diagnosed with rheumatic fever and admitted to the hospital. There I was alone again, but with nice nurses looking after me, bringing me food regularly, giving me back rubs. Best of all was a TV that got more channels than we got at home. When I was discharged, we were told that I could not return to school for the rest of the year. Part of me was relieved. Once again, though, I was left alone when my mother went to work and my brother went to school. She set up a bed on the couch and put a TV stand next to the couch with bread and butter and a toaster on it. I was told not to get up, not to go upstairs to my room, not to exert myself; I could only go to the bathroom and get something to drink. I had to take my own temperature and pulse and call it in to the doctor's office every day. I was alone with the TV and my thoughts.

Even though I had a mother and adults around me, I could see that I was on my own. It was a lesson I carried for many years.

4

Isolation Is Familiar

Alone at night
I wondered why.

Hot summer nights alone in my room,
the heat of the attic
coaxed at the old, ugly wallpaper
so it hung loosely from the wall.
The smell of old glue floated in the air.

Alone at night.

I thought I saw Indian people.
They had no faces,
they had no bodies,
but they were there.

Standing there looking at me as I lay there,
as if they were whispering something to me.

Just when I thought I might hear them,
the quiet of the room shouted over their voices.

"Don't you remember you are alone? They didn't want you."

Then the Indians left.
And I was in my room alone again,
alone beyond knowing.

I hoped they would come again.

Alone at night
I wondered why.

ALL THE OTHER GIRLS at the Reedsburg high school had short hair. They seemed to like it. So I figured out how to make it work and I kept my feelings inside—how I felt like a boy. I reached a compromise that would keep my mom off my back: almost-shoulder-length hair. As a young teenager I washed and set my hair every night. In a solitary ritual, I first stood in front of the mirror, trying to braid my almost-long-enough hair. Why? I don't know. I wanted the braids, but I wouldn't have worn them. I was too scared, no one else wore them, and I couldn't explain why I wanted them.

The perfectly formed white girls, with their thin, blond hair and their milky white skin, gave me sneering looks. The boys stared at them and wanted them. I almost wanted to be white, because I would at least be noticed. I almost wanted it, maybe even wanted it for a moment, as I stood at my gym locker, ashamed of my not-completely-brown-not-completely-white skin, with a little stomach pouch that most Indian girls have. All I knew was that my body was not like the white girls', and those girls took great joy in pointing that out any time they thought I may have forgotten it.

When I walked down the street of my hometown, a car would drive by and I would hear the Hollywood war whoop, or "Hey, squaw," or "How about some firewater, squaw?" It stung. The one time I told my adoptive mom, she said, "I don't know why they would do that. You don't look Indian. You don't even have black hair." I don't look Indian? How could she say that? I did not look white. What did I look like? I knew. I looked ugly, and that was all I needed to know. I was a misfit who had to learn to make do. Survive. I was alone in this.

The announcements at our homecoming pep rally had said, "We need everyone to come help with the freshman float." So I went to the float-making in the big room across the street from Phil's Cozy Corner. The girls stared. Not one said, "We're glad you're here. We need the extra hands." So I left.

A little later in the night, they had the Snake Dance. I didn't talk to anyone, but I participated, holding hands in a chain of what seemed like hundreds of kids on the sidewalks. The first in line led the "snake chain" of giggling, howling youth through stores, through alleys, and down Main Street. We screamed and laughed as we held on to each other's hands, not wanting to break the chain. I was part of it, but I enjoyed it alone.

I stood at the side at the homecoming dance and watched the girls dance with their boyfriends. I liked the music. I liked some of the outfits the girls wore. I wanted to talk to someone about what I saw, but I was alone.

The school play was *L'il Abner*, and I went to it alone. The actors demonstrated such ease, and I wanted to do it, too, but I was afraid to go try out. I was not pretty like them, nor did anyone really seem to notice that I existed.

From junior high on, I roller-skated every Sunday. I felt free on skates. I could skate backward easily. I could two-step, schottische, and waltz without missing a beat. The boys wanted to skate with me because I could skate. It felt good. I loved roller-skating.

It was a winter night. I sat on the passenger side in the back seat of a '55 Chevy wearing a white tent dress with animal-print faux-fur cuffs. I was smoking a Marlboro and drinking blackberry brandy in a Styrofoam cup. It sweetly and tartly stung my tongue. As I drank it, I felt it go to my veins, then to my head. It felt like I was home. I fell in love and chased this elusive lover for fourteen years.

I don't know exactly how it started, but I did find some friends. They seemed to like me. They were mostly older than me. The boys had a car. The girls liked to drink with them. I heard that they were "hoods." I liked how they walked into a room like they owned it, when I knew full well how others who thought they were better looked down on them.

And so, to numb the pain and confusion of the hard times, I started drinking at the age of fourteen and taking drugs at sixteen. Being drunk and stoned made me feel like someone, like I had an identity. Somehow being a drinking, cussing party girl who could hang with the boys gave me the strength I needed to get by, so that became my identity. I didn't have anything else.

I managed to graduate from high school, earned an AA degree, joined the navy, got married, had two children, got sober, and then got divorced.

Through it all, I remembered the single piece of information I had about my Indian mother that suggested maybe I was more than a welfare check to spend on booze. That story from my adoptive mother had only one line in it, and I only heard it a couple of times. "Your mother used to come and sit in the back of the church so you wouldn't see her."

I knew better than to show any excitement at hearing this. That would arouse fear that would quickly turn to rage in my adoptive mother. I just thought, *She came to see me? That must have been because she needed to see that I was okay.* I hung on to that one-sentence story, not having any words to describe why. Hope was something I could not express or cling to. I just held my breath, longing to hear the words again: *"Your mother used to come and sit in the back of the church so you wouldn't see her."*

It is true that my Indian mother drank. Maybe I have compassion for her because I have been a drunken mother. I am well acquainted with the painful feelings of inadequacy and the shame of not being able to be the mother I wanted to be because alcohol called and I followed. It was, after all, my one true, trusted lover, the only thing I could count on to calm the noise in my head and give me the confidence I was so desperately looking for. *"Your mother used to come and sit in the back of the church so you wouldn't see her."*

My adoptive mother sat with me in the front of the church. When she knew my Indian mother was in the back of the church, did she feel self-righteous, thinking that this was what this woman gets for being a drunken Indian? Was she scared that my Indian mom might approach her and want me back? When I squirmed in the pew, as toddlers do, and looked to the back of the church, did her heart race nervously, fearing that I'd see my mother and want to return to those familiar brown arms? Did she pray for the health and happiness of my mother, have any pity for her and how our people were treated? *"Your mother used to come and sit in the back of the church so you wouldn't see her."*

Did my Indian mother look at me, wanting to cry? Did her heart race nervously as she watched me squirm in the pew, as toddlers do? Was she afraid or hopeful that our eyes would meet and I would recognize her and want to run to her arms? Did she see me and smile with that mother's satisfaction and love that there are no words for? Did she wish she could have me back? Did seeing me with my adoptive mom make her feel inadequate and ashamed? Was she secretly relieved to be rid of the responsibility of taking care of me, so she could answer the call to that elusive lover, alcohol? Did she hope and pray that someday I'd be okay, healthy, and proud to be a Lakota woman? Did anyone offer her any comfort as she watched her once-daughter with another family? *"Your mother used to come and sit in the back of the church so you wouldn't see her."*

In 1994, I was at my brother's house in Winner. One day while exploring, I drove down the dirt road behind his house. Near the end of the road was an old church. I slowed down. Could this be the church I heard my adoptive mother talk about? I drove into the parking lot looking at the church with a distant yet familiar feeling. A caretaker happened to be there, and I asked if this church was in existence in the 1950s and was Virginia Ladd a member? She was the woman who supposedly found out about me and let the church Indians know. The caretaker said, "Yes, this is the church."

I told him that I was from Wisconsin and visiting my brother who lived down the road. We shook hands, and I said, "I used to go to church here when I was small. Could I go in?"

"Sure, go on in," he said.

I turned, walked up the few wooden stairs, opened the

door, and stepped just inside. I looked around at the small room, then sat in the last pew, in the back of the church. I caressed the wood, remembering how hard these pews were during long sermons. I spent the first half of my life in churches. These pews had that familiar old-wood smell.

I imagined my Indian mother sitting in this very spot, watching me. Here she watched as her brown baby grew away from her. I remembered being taken into the parking lot to be spanked because I could not sit still and be quiet. No amount of soda crackers could suppress my desire to move and talk. My adoptive father's large, thick hands hit my bottom and lifted me off the ground with each blow. The gravel crunched under his heavy feet, the sun shone hot, and I sobbed. I didn't have words for this then, but it stands out so vivid in my mind.

I was once the brown baby in the front of this church. Here I sit now, the grown brown woman in the very place my Indian mother sat.

The Indian baby grew to be a strong Indian woman. She sits in the back of the church, a proud Lakota wiŋyaŋ (woman). I have learned the Creator sees through our bargaining, our misguided requests, our self-righteous and fearful requests, and honors our heart's desire. Often His gifts are not in the package we want, but they are the gifts we deserve and need. So it was with the prayers of my two wounded mothers. Their wounded prayers were answered through the unfolding of my life.

A few years after I met my Indian family, I began writing down my thoughts about my life. Someone had said to me, "You have to forgive your mother." I grimaced internally at the thought. How could I forgive her? She was so hateful. As a baby I turned from her attempts at affection, an innocent and normal fear of a stranger. My mother internalized my fear of her as rejection. My rejection and revulsion intensified as the abuse wore on. My rejection of her affection became permanent as it was fueled by her rage, slaps, and sexual abuse.

My Indian mother had no resources.

My adoptive mother had no resources.

I absorbed all that was absent in their lives and became their wounds and pains personified. I prayed. I asked Creator, "Can I forgive her, just between You and me, and not to her face?" I just did not have the strength to separate myself from the past. Whenever I spent time with her, I would become dark and emotionless.

In 1994, I got a phone call. My adoptive mother was in the hospital and most likely not going to live through the night. The nurse wanted to know if I would be coming to see her one last time. I asked about her condition. The nurse said something about her heart and that she was not in pain but not going to make it much longer and was resting well right now.

I took a deep breath, flooded with the memories of the many times as a child that my adoptive mother would put the fear of death in me—the fear of *her* death.

Her hysterical crying rang in my ears. "You don't care anyway; all you think of is yourself. I could die and you wouldn't care. I have a heart condition; I could die any time! Then you'll be sorry." Those words slapped my face, leaving the ooze of shame that stuck to my chest, making it hard to breathe. I was numb with fear.

I wanted nothing more than *not* to be responsible for making her feel so miserable. I used to feel so sorry for her at times. It wasn't hard to feel sorry for her, because she was so pitiful. Of course I was to blame, because I was such an ungrateful daughter. I tried so hard to be the perfect white Christian girl. No matter what I did, I always was reminded that I was Indian, and that meant that I was never good enough. Except when it meant my mother could look good for her sacrifice in rescuing me from the reservation.

I pictured her lying there in the hospital bed. I hadn't seen her in several years. She had called me once to tell me she was sick and hospitalized. I told her that I would pray for her and that I knew God would provide the support she needed. He always had. My mother had become quite resourceful and strangely connected to people, much more than she had been when I was a child.

In 1972, I had felt forced to visit her at the Reedsburg hospital. I carried the heavy "I am an ungrateful daughter" mantle on my shoulders as I walked through the hospital doors. I only broke from my partying because I received a phone call from a family friend. "You need to go see your mother. She's pretty sick." More out of respect for this family friend than concern or desire to see my mother, I made the trip back to Reedsburg.

I had moved to Madison, sixty miles south of Reedsburg. Finally, I had some distance between me and that madness. Living in the big city, I was a party girl. That meant that I drank hard, did drugs, and hung out with musicians. My life could be summed up in the words: *sex, drugs, and rock 'n' roll.* I was a self-supporting drug dealer. Before this lifestyle got the best of me, I had some exceptionally fun times. I was proud of myself.

Even though the mantle of shame was heavy, I mustered up my newfound inner strength and identity and made the trip. I don't remember what we said during the visit. I had stopped hearing her voice—a defense mechanism. She lay there with that look on her face. That pained look of despair that reminded me of how I contributed to her illness.

Living on my own in Madison, I began to feel a little better about myself. Even if it was a drunken identity, it was an identity nonetheless, and it seemed better and separate from the mantle my mother gave me. It certainly was more fun. I found my style—Frye boots and jeans. My life was a full schedule of bars and drugs. I tried to go to college, but basically majored in drinking and partying. Most students live their lives around their class schedule. I lived my life around the bar schedule. There was Tuesday night pitcher night at El Tejon,

Wednesday night tequila night at Bachelors III, and Thursday night Stone Hearth. Then there was Friday and Saturday, and they were party nights just because it was Friday and Saturday. I generally took Sunday off. Well, maybe not from full-on partying—I stayed home and got high. Life was good in my deluded, addicted mind.

I remembered the screaming, the slaps, and ducking thrown objects. And her cruelest form of abuse: a complete rejection of my natural spirit.

All these thoughts whirled as the nurse waited for my response. I said calmly, "No, I won't be coming to see her. Has my brother been there?"

"Yes," replied the nurse. "As I said, your mother is resting comfortably right now but we don't expect her to make it through the night."

"That is good my brother is there," I responded flatly.

The nurse said, "We'll call you if anything changes."

I hung up the phone. I was quiet. I was in shock. Not at the prospect of losing my adoptive mother. It seemed to me as if I lost her many years before. I had grieved her already, as I began separating from all the years of mental and physical abuse. As a child I knew that she could die any day, and it would be my fault because I was such an ungrateful, selfish daughter. She said her heart was bad. She spent mysterious times in the hospital for "rest." Now it was some twenty-five years later, and at age eighty-four, she was finally passing into the spirit world.

When my mother had her "spells," she must have felt like she was dying. If she suffered from undiagnosed and untreated mental illness, she must have truly suffered in the isolation of the illness and anxiety that made her so repulsive to me and others.

The next morning, the nurse called again and spoke in a slow, quiet, kind, professional voice. "She went comfortably."

She went comfortably—how could she have gone comfortably, when she lived so uncomfortably? It was Saturday morning, wash day. I had my usual two weeks' worth, fifteen loads of laundry. I began the long process of carrying the five heaping baskets of laundry downstairs, loading them into my car, and then lugging them each into the laundromat. I sorted the loads into piles in front of the washing machine, and then one by one dropped my quarters into each machine. As I sat down to wait, I realized what had been on my mind.

I was thinking about all the times as a child I was afraid my mother would die and it would be my fault. I was recalling all the fights, the yelling, her crying, me crying. I thought of the times she was nice to me and it would feel good, but never for very long. With each memory it seemed as if I was putting that past in the washer.

Wouldn't it be so nice if we could put our troubles, worries, hurts, and pains into a washing machine and have them washed, rinsed, and wrung out? And then whatever emotional bacteria was left would die in the heat of the dryer?

Permanent press.

Cottons.

Denims.

Whites.

Colors.

It was symbolic for me. As I sorted the darks from the whites, loaded each washer, dropped my coins in, pushed the wash cycle, I began to think of the five things I learned from my mother.

● There is a God. She did not introduce me to a loving God, but I learned there was a God and discovered on my own the loving God of grace.

● I can be independent. After my dad died, she never remarried. She maintained our household, kept her car running, and did all the other things a woman of her age typically relied on a man for. This taught me that I did not need a man to survive.

● I learned a work ethic. She abandoned me to go to work, but she consistently went to work every day, never abusing her sick days. She honestly cared for the elders she looked after in the nursing home. She told us many stories about them, until my brother and I felt they were a part of our lives.

● I deserve good mental health. She thought I was a "nervous wreck" and sent me to counselors who had no idea how to help a transracially adopted child who was, in fact, struggling with the trauma of separation. Even though the professionals didn't help me, I somehow got the message that I deserved good mental health care.

● She taught me what a child needs by not being able to mother me. All that I did not receive from her, I tried to give my children, and in doing that, I healed myself.

Life with her was difficult, and it took years to undo the hurt. But I did learn valuable life lessons from her. I made peace in the laundromat; the heat of the dryer killed the remaining bacteria. "She went comfortably" was her final blessing. My blessings were just beginning.

PART 2

Healing

5

Wings on a Dream

THERE ARE PEOPLE who the Creator chooses to be a part of your dream. That is what Susan Bender and Ralph Swaboda were in my life. It was the middle of July 1989, and I was still unable to work. The disability payment I was finally receiving for my CFS was barely enough to meet bills and pay my subsidized rent. Now that it was summer, my thoughts were back on Rosebud, recalling the urging of my relatives who said, "You should come back over Rosebud Fair. That's when everyone comes home." I had talked and talked about wanting to go to South Dakota again, but I had no financial means to do so. My heart ached to return.

Susan was bringing my son back after some playtime at her house with her son. I saw her pull into our parking lot, and I walked down to meet them. She handed me a small envelope. I opened it, and inside there was $200 in a blank card that had a handwritten note saying, "Time to put wings on your dream." I knew the dream meant to go to South Dakota. Susan then said she'd watch my children while I traveled.

It was a warm, sunny July day. A light breeze blew across my cheek as if the Creator was caressing my face, saying, "I know your heart's desires, my girl. I will always take care of you." I was left without words. I hugged Susan and thanked her, knowing there was no way to pay her back—other than always to remember her in my prayers.

Once again, I was making my way west by the Creator's hand. I was going to be at the Rosebud Fair.

I called my aunt Cecilia and told her I was coming with a friend, and asked her if we could stay at her house. She said sure. Then I was off to another life-changing adventure.

By this time, I had learned that the Rosebud Indian Reservation is the home of the Sicangu Lakota Oyate. *Sicangu* means "burnt thigh"; *oyate* means "the people." The Lakota are one of the Seven Council Fires, the Oceti Sakowin—the people often known as the Sioux.

We made it to the reservation and found my aunt's trailer in Mission, a small town on the reservation. When we entered her cozy trailer, she was there with her daughter Baby C, short for Baby Cecilia, to differentiate her from her mother. My aunt Cecilia is named after my grandmother Cecilia, and she then named her daughter Cecilia. Baby C explained that if she too had a girl, she would name her Cecilia. Many Indian families name their children after family members, and the child is often affectionately stuck with the "Baby," even into adulthood. You could visit any reservation and hear someone say, "Do you mean Roger or Baby Roger?" and Baby Roger is forty-five!

After my friend and I settled our things into the back room that my aunt had prepared for us, we went to the living room to visit. My aunt told us how to get to the powwow grounds and explained that my uncles would be at the softball games that were right next to the grounds. She also told me that my aunt Norma, Uncle Manfred's wife, had a restaurant in a trailer set up at the powwow grounds. She said, "You'll see the sign, Norma's Cafe. Stop in there to see your uncle."

That night my friend and I settled in to share the double bed. As I lay there, I said to her, "I know I just got here, but I feel so comfortable. Why is that?"

"Because it's your family," she said. I did not have a response. I just rolled the comment around in my head. *Because it's your family.*

The next morning Aunt Cecilia fixed us breakfast. She told us it was going to be really hot and we might want to wait until later in the day to go to the powwow. So we settled into the living room, enjoying the window air conditioner and watching MTV. Later in the afternoon, Aunt Cecilia said she would give us a ride to the powwow, and when we were ready to come home, we should call her and she'd come pick us up. I got ready to go to my first Rosebud Fair, which includes a carnival, softball tournament, powwow, and rodeo all at the same time, side by side. We decided to get dropped by the café first. My uncle Terry and my uncle Clifford were both in the café eating lunch. They smiled and said they were glad that I came home again. They told me about the construction company they owned, Fast Horse Construction. It made me feel proud to know they were not only laborers but businessmen as well.

I asked my uncles if anyone had a picture of my mother. None of them did. What pictures they had were burned in home fires. Just then one of my cousins came into the café. After she was introduced to me, my uncle said, "One of your mother's cousins, Doris Fallis, might have pictures of your mother."

Dieta, my newly found cousin, said, "Doris is probably down at Ghost Hawk Park." It was where our tribal college, Sinte Gleska, holds its graduation.

My friend and I piled into someone's car with Dieta and rode down to Ghost Hawk Park, about seven miles from Norma's Café. On the way, she said she had thought I was Deborah, my sister. She said she remembered Deborah and three other siblings, including another younger brother. She smiled and said he used to love to sing "Jesus Loves Me." Those missionaries, they just got to everyone!

We pulled into Ghost Hawk Park, an area full of trees, picnic tables, and families. There, my cousin introduced me to Doris Fallis. When Doris heard who I was, she smiled big and hugged me. Then she took my hand and wrapped it around her forearm. We began walking slowly as she spoke and patted my hand. "I used to watch you when you were a baby when your mother went on her 'adventures.' Your mother"—she paused and took a long breath—"your mother was adventurous"—she looked off—"and would leave you with me."

I told Doris it was okay, that I knew my mother drank and that I was not mad or ashamed. "I am a recovering alcoholic myself," I assured her.

I listened to Doris recall her times with me. She stopped once and looked at me, smiled, and said, "You had blond hair when you were a baby." I laughed at that thought, only to find out later that many of us are born with blond hair that turns black by toddlerhood. It felt so good to be close to someone, a relative who had held me and taken care of me and could tell me about it. I stopped at Doris's house before I went back to Madison, and she gave me pictures of my mother.

The next day, a tall, young man walked into my aunt's trailer. He introduced himself: "Hi, I'm your uncle Art."

After some conversation, I had to ask him, "So, do you remember me as a baby?"

"Yes," he replied. "I used to get stuck babysitting all the young kids."

"Wow," I said. "You babysat me? Was I a cute baby?" I hoped maybe he'd tell me what I was like as a baby.

In a very matter-of-fact tone he said, without even looking at me, "No, you was ugly." I knew he was teasing, and we laughed hard together. I liked him immediately.

I met other cousins and relatives during the days of the powwow. I began to feel that I belonged there, and when it was time to go back to Madison, it was hard to leave.

I returned to Madison filled with more of a sense of who I was than ever before. Susan had looked after my children, as she said she would. I felt guilty about not bringing them with me, but I needed the time to myself to explore this new territory. It was all so new to me, and I knew I could not take everything in and take care of all their curiosities at the same time. As I drove to Susan's house to pick them up, I told myself it was okay they did not make this trip with me and that someday they would meet their relatives, too. After the kids and I hugged and kissed hello, they went back to playing so I could tell Susan about my visit.

I filled her in on all the details, then brought out the pictures of my mother. I had only looked at them briefly. Sitting at Susan's kitchen breakfast bar, I got lost staring at one of them. I heard her say, "You look like your mother," and she even saw similarities in my children. Then it hit me. I looked at the picture of my mother and began to cry. Then I got mad, really mad, and began to breathe hard. I felt like running somewhere, anywhere.

I went out to my car and found the small package of loose tobacco that someone had given me when they showed me how to pray with tobacco.* "Keep it with you at all times," they said as they handed it to me, "you never know when you'll need it." I had placed it in the glove box, not realizing just how significant this gift was. I took the tobacco and walked behind Susan's house. She lived in an upscale rural housing development. Her house sat on a hill, the backyard edged with trees facing west. I walked behind the trees to an open spot looking out on the small valley.

The sun was beginning its daily journey below the horizon, bathing the panoramic view with soft, golden light. I opened the package of tobacco, took a small pinch as I had been shown, and placed it in my left hand. I stood there with the tobacco in my hand, looking up into the sky. I began by saying, "You made me Indian. I don't even know what

---

*Tobacco is a sacred plant given to us by the Creator; it is offered in prayer and as a communion with earth, water, and sky and between nations or individuals. Offerings are given to maintain balance and order. When we ask something of someone, we give something back to maintain balance.

My mother, Nina Lulu White Hawk Garneaux, probably 1960s

it means to be Indian. You let me live way over here. All I know is the white way. From now on, I want you to talk to me like I am an Indian woman. I don't even know any Indians; don't even have an Indian friend." I was so mad and hurt all at once, but mostly I remember the anger. My throat pulled and ached, and I sobbed in frustration. I put the tobacco down on the ground and walked back to the house wondering, *What's next?*

It seemed so cruel to be taken from a family who wanted to keep me, only to be raised by an abusive white mother. Now I was divorced, I had lost a house in the process, and I was sick with something most people didn't even understand. Many people, even friends, doubted that I was really sick. Most thought I was depressed or exaggerating whatever illness I had. It was like that day in school when no one wanted to believe I was sick. Once again, I had something that you couldn't see on the outside. Once again, I was surrounded by doubting faces and disrespectful comments.

Returning to Madison put me right back in all the hard challenges of my life. And sometimes they bit me when I wasn't expecting it.

It seems that I always have a box of papers to go through. I try to organize, but alas, I have not reached the goal of having everything in its place.

I was going through one of them in 1990. The box was full of papers and a few photos from when I was married. I had forgotten all about these professional pictures. I shuffled slowly through the pictures, smiling at the faces of my babies. Memories of what they were like at that age, three and nine, danced in my mind. I looked at their innocent faces and prayed for their hearts to flourish, even though we were on this path into single motherhood with very little money. I held each picture and smiled, remembering the smell of their sweaty heads after they played outside on a hot summer day. I loved being a mother, even though I felt like I was making it up as I went along.

Then I shuffled to another picture and there we were, a family. A dad, a mom, and two children, one boy, one girl; the perfect nuclear family. I stared at the picture, recalling the state of my relationship with my now ex-husband. We were all smiling. But I was smiling through years of abusive arguments with a cheating husband, an alcoholic who, despite repeated efforts, would not get sober. The children were too small to know anything about that. They just knew they loved their daddy, so I tried to preserve that for them—at great cost to my own mental health.

One last picture, a posed color photo. I was standing behind my ex-husband with my hands on his shoulders. I wore a white cotton blouse with eyelet lace and black slacks. I thought, *I wish I could still tuck my shirt in like that!* My husband was wearing a blue suit and smiling big like he was really happy. I looked again and noticed they touched up the photo and took off the watch I was wearing. I looked again at my face. *I hate my smile. My hair looks okay, but it's too poofy and curly*—the popular look at the time. I pretended I liked it, but I was always extremely uncomfortable with it. I looked again, and then suddenly I gasped and turned the picture over and laid it on the counter.

I looked to see if anyone had heard me, but I was alone. I turned over the photo again, and once again was startled and laid the picture facedown on the counter. This time I took a deep breath and said in a prayer, "What is going on? What is wrong?" My heart was racing, and I felt like I wanted to stare at something I shouldn't be looking at. The image seemed almost three-dimensional to me.

Once again, I turned over the photo. I noticed that my skin was a little browner than usual, as the picture was taken at the end of summer. I always spend as much time as possible at the beach with the kids. *What is it about this picture?* I stared again and slowly the words came from someplace way back in my consciousness. I heard the words faintly at first, then loudly. "Oh my God, I'm not white!" I said out loud. I looked around again as if someone would hear me. I looked back at the picture and saw my skin, my brown skin against the white skin of my ex.

I saw my brown skin. Why was I so shocked? *What is the big deal?* I thought. *Come on now, you're brown; your ex is white—big deal.*

But there were solid reasons for my surprising reaction.

When a baby is born, his presence brings joy, excitement, and the hope that family names will be carried on. His mother holds him and stares into his face. His father holds him and stares into his face. Then, Mom and Dad look at each other in disbelief and happiness. The first few hours of a baby's life draw everyone to stare into this innocent face of purity. A few months later, the baby can be held at arm's length, or up in the air, while the adult stares into the baby's face. This is done so often psychologists call it *mirroring*. The parents' mirroring responses influence the development and maintenance of self-esteem and self-assertive ambitions. Their response will mirror back to the child a sense of worth, which in turn creates an internal self-respect.

This mirroring process is innate. We don't think about it. Both parties engage, and it feeds the mind and the psyche. When you're young, you innocently think you look like the face you have been staring into for all your life. I remember when I first spent time in front of the mirror by myself. It was very uncomfortable. I didn't think much about it as I grew up, but as time went on I have figured this out.

When someone does not look like the other one in the mirroring process, they'll shift their image of themselves until they believe they look like those around them, including their community. I was the only Indian girl in the town I grew up in. No one looked like me. I did not see my image reflected in my family or my community. I erased my face so that I did not feel uncomfortable when I looked in the mirror. I recall one time when someone commented to my adoptive mother, "Sandy even looks like you." So it was confirmed to me: I looked white. My adoptive mother even reinforced this, telling me, "You don't look Indian. If you were Indian, your hair would be black, but your hair is brown." Unconsciously, I rearranged my image to fit my surroundings. It worked—until I went home to the reservation.

There, I encountered my biological mirror in my relatives. I stared at them as if I was staring into my face for the first time. I loved their smiles, their teeth, their hair. Now back in my apartment, as I looked at these pictures, I began to rewire my reality. I could see my brown skin, my black hair, my teeth. It took me a while to get used to this.

This awareness all came out of the drawer where I put things that I don't know what to do with. I knew I was Indian, but I had to tuck it away because it made those around me uncomfortable.

And CFS didn't help my stressful situation. I visited a friend who worked as an alcohol and drug counselor. After I was introduced to his coworkers, one asked the usual question: "What do you do?" I had not yet practiced my slick comebacks and answered by saying, "Nothing right now. I'm recovering from chronic fatigue syndrome."

He sarcastically replied, "I wish I could lie around all day. It must be nice to do that and get paid for it." I was frozen, unable to speak. This was the first time I heard that kind of comment.

But the next time I heard it, I was ready. I responded with, "No, you wouldn't like to lie around all day. We're not meant to lie around day. It's not like resting. It is like being sick every day and having to rest because you're weak, except you don't get better and you don't get your energy back. I don't think you'd like it."

It seemed like I had no life, only survival. I was tired of surviving. I wanted to live. Was my life ever going to be without cruelty and disappointment? I began to walk through an incredibly difficult time, a time filled with doubt, confusion, purging of memories, and working to change my belief in myself. For at least a year, I woke up every day angry, so angry that I would have fingernail marks in the palms of my hands.

I had been to the reservation twice and started feeling torn about living in Madison. Now I had family to miss, a land to miss. Many, many memories were surfacing that I had to work through. It seemed endless, like my life was never going to be normal, whatever that meant.

All I knew to do was go to my 12-step meetings and talk to my support people. Every day I got up, went outside, put tobacco down, and prayed. I prayed about my anger and my finances—and I asked for help.

I was sitting in the waiting room at the garage, waiting for an oil change. It was a typical auto shop waiting room filled with grease and oil smells, and I was trying to find something interesting in one of the outdated magazines when an older man with white hair struck up a conversation. He asked me about the jacket I was wearing. It had the logo of Little Hoop Treatment facility on it. My uncles had given it to me when they told me their construction company built the facility in a small town on the reservation.

Why did I wear this? I thought to myself. I did not wear it to invite conversation. I liked wearing it because it made me feel close to my family in Rosebud.

"Are you from South Dakota?" he asked.

"I was born on the Rosebud Reservation," I replied, hoping he wouldn't ask me any other questions.

"I see your jacket has the name of a treatment center," he pressed. "I'm a friend of Bill W." Saying you are a friend of Bill W. is a public way for someone to say they are in recovery and to see if the person they are speaking with also knows Bill W. This is considered a safe way to find out if someone attends 12-step meetings.

"Me, too," I said with an internal sigh, bracing myself for questions about being Indian that I could not answer. Then he began telling me that he was a salesman who had spent years traveling in northern Wisconsin, and that he had attended 12-step meetings close to the reservations and had met many recovering Indian people.

"I was always touched by their spirituality. It is so simple and so powerful. I miss those meetings," he said with a kind recollection.

I sat and looked at this white man who wanted to strike up a conversation with an Indian. I was so angry and just did not want to talk to any more white people. I spent all my life with white people. Now I wanted to be with Indian people. And here I was, faced with this typical, neatly dressed white man with tasseled loafers and fancy socks. I do not recall what I told him about myself. I do remember saying, "I have been sober for nine years now, and it seems my life is still fucked up. The only difference is that I am sober through it."

He listened with compassion in his eyes. It almost made me uncomfortable, as I was still trying to get used to people being compassionate. After I was done talking, I looked down, feeling somewhat embarrassed. *Why do I do this? I talk too much,* I scolded myself.

Then he said, "Sounds like you're disillusioned with your sobriety. It happens to a lot of us, especially around the ten-year mark. We alcoholics often falsely believe that life should be different for us. That we should not have any of life's struggles, especially after we get sober. Everyone has things in life that are difficult at times. If you focus on the things in your life you are grateful for, this disillusionment will disappear."

Just then the man behind the counter said, "White Hawk!" indicating my car was done. I shook the older man's hand, thanked him for his words, and went to pick up my keys.

It was one of those times when the Creator's hand had given me exactly what I needed exactly when I needed it, even in the midst of my cynicism, anger, and resentment. I have often counted this blessing in my gratitude list. The Creator used this nameless friend of Bill W. to soften the pain, to give me strength to go on, to renew hope, to turn anger into gratitude.

Not long after this encounter, I was at my usual 12-step meeting, and there was a new person, a woman who looked to me to be either Mexican or Hawaiian. I listened with interest as she talked about the topic of the meeting. She also mentioned that she was from the Menominee Reservation, and that she had a lot of anger toward white people and was working on it. I could sure relate to that! She talked about the principles of the program and her desire to let go of negativity. She sounded like she was on a good path.

After the meeting, she introduced herself to me. She told me later that her sponsor told her to do this because I had ten years of sobriety. I told her that if she ever needed a ride to a meeting, she could call me, and we exchanged phone numbers.

We became friends. I shared what I learned about sobriety and encouraged her to know that she could recover with the promise to be "happy, joyous, and free" (although not entirely without problems!). I began visiting the Menominee Reservation with her. It is a beautiful place full of lush forest. The Menominee people I met were gracious, generous people who provided me with a sense of home when I was so far away from it. I told Uncle Manfred about the Menominee Reservation's beautiful powwow grounds, built in a natural bowl, and how the dancers danced under the ancient trees.

But the most life-changing aspect of our friendship was that she introduced me to the Madison Indian community. I had lived in Madison since 1972. After eighteen years, I had no idea there was an Indian community. I began looking in the events section of the *Isthmus* newspaper, and I saw a listing for a Native American speaker at the university. I decided to go.

Nick Hockings, a tall brown man, stood in the front of the university classroom preparing to make his presentation. Students were entering the room, passing me as I slowly walked toward a seat, looking at Nick at the same time. The smell of chalk and old wood filled the air, and I tried not to stare but couldn't help myself. I was thirty-six years old and, aside from my Indian family in South Dakota, he was about the third Indian I had ever seen. It was hard to keep my eyes off his frame, his long hair, and the beadwork on his vest. I finally found a seat among all the white students. Afraid of appearing rude and intrusive, and worried he might get the wrong impression, I shifted my gaze to the top of my desk. I took a deep breath, trying not to appear anxious or excited. I did not know anyone in the room. Nevertheless, it just felt so good to see a brown person, especially in the front of the classroom as a presenter. I didn't feel as alone as I usually did.

He introduced himself in Ojibwe and then in English. He was from the Lac du Flambeau Reservation in Wisconsin. He talked about his involvement in exercising his fishing rights. In northern Wisconsin during the late 1980s and early 1990s, whites and Indians were deeply divided on the treaty rights of the Ojibwe to spearfish outside of the state-designated fishing season. Spearfishing was a way of life for the Ojibwe; it was their heritage. I listened intently as he explained the spiritual connection to the water, the fish, and the seasonal ceremony that took place, including a feast of the speared fish. He told about how this way of life keeps the Ojibwe people strong.

He described how they prayed and sang before they fished. How they prayed for the men and women who would be jeering at them from the fishing docks. They withstood racial slurs. Some of the protestors carried signs that said, "Spear an Indian, save a walleye." He said that he and the other men were scared, but nevertheless they needed to do this. They needed to exercise their rights, the rights their ancestors had worked so hard to preserve in all the treaties that took their land. They also needed to spearfish for their children and the generation yet to come. He and the others took their protective medicines, called upon their ancestors to protect them, and walked through the wall of hostile, angry white people, some shouting death threats. Quietly, he and the others got into their boats and rowed out to fish. At that moment, out there in the boat with his back turned toward the shore, he realized that he could be killed.

The white people there did not understand the Ojibwe way of life. They did not know that the Ojibwe people would not take more than they needed. And mostly they did not understand the importance of taking fish at that time of year, outside of the state's fishing season. I listened, wishing I could have been there to support those brave individuals who honored their ancestors and gave hope to the future generations.

I wasn't Ojibwe, but I understood. I didn't grow up with Indian people, but I understood. I was proud to be Lakota but ashamed that I didn't know more. I was encouraged by his story.

Nick then went into talking about his childhood and his recovery from alcoholism. He spoke so openly, assuredly, and humbly. I understood the struggle of getting comfortable with sobriety. This quiet man who so openly shared his life experiences touched me in a way that I had to acknowledge. I wasn't quite sure why, but I felt better about *me* by listening to him. It had been only a year since I had connected with my Lakota relatives. I wanted to talk to him, to tell him that he gave me hope. It seemed I *needed* to talk to someone, anyone, or I would burst.

When the presentation ended, I waited until everyone left and Nick was standing alone. Shyly, I approached him. I introduced myself and told him that I really liked what he had to say and that it made me feel good. I told him that I was from the Rosebud Indian Reservation but was adopted out as a toddler and raised there in Wisconsin. I told him that just last year I found my Indian family. I don't know what I said to him after that. I just remember words were falling out of my mouth, tumbling into the air in confusion and sadness.

I wanted what he had. He knew who he was. He knew some of his language. He knew songs. He knew the ceremonies. He had confidence in his life as an Ojibwe man. All I could say was, "I am from Rosebud." I wanted to know more and I wanted to know more *now!* I wanted him to tell me something, anything. I wanted him to reassure me. He was Indian.

He patiently listened to me with his eyes fixed on the floor, his brown hands gently clasped over each other in front of him. He nodded as I told him that I had been adopted out and that I had just met my family. He told me how happy he was that I was finding out more about my identity. I said more and then ran out of words. We stood there in silence for a moment. He raised his head, and with a gentle voice, he said, "This path you are on now, you are right where you are supposed to be. Things will come as you need them."

What? Right where I am supposed to be? What? Didn't he hear me? Couldn't he tell I needed more than that? My mind reeled. But I faked a smile and shook his outstretched hand.

But what in the world did he mean? I am right where I am supposed to be? It did not seem that way to me. I was on a path that felt foreign, that felt uncomfortable, that I did not want to be on. Even though I met my family, I still felt so disconnected. I was not where I was supposed be. I was still far away from where I wanted to be. But how could he know that? He grew up with his people. He knew his place. He knew songs and ceremonies, and he knew how to spearfish.

All I knew was that I was from Rosebud and that I had a large Indian family. I didn't know any songs or ceremonies, how to dance, or anything like that. How could it be possible that I was right where I was supposed to be?

I walked out of the building with him, not wanting to say goodbye. When we got to his car, he reached in and took out a map. He told me about an upcoming veterans' powwow on a reservation in northern Wisconsin. I didn't say I was too shy to go to a powwow. I just looked at the map with him as he explained where it was.

He shook my hand and said, "See you again. Indians don't say goodbye; most Indian languages don't have a word for goodbye. We say, 'see you again,' because we will see each other again."

He got in his car and I waved as he drove away. *See you again,* I thought to myself. Somehow it was easier this way, knowing that I would see him again, sometime, somewhere.

I look back at this interaction and see how healing it was. His just being who he was quieted my anxious spirit. I did see

Nick Hockings again, many times. He was a frequent visitor in Madison. Years later, after I began powwow dancing, I even got to dance with him with the Call for Peace Dance Troupe.

That path that I was on then is the same path I am on today. I have just traveled farther. Then, I was right where I was supposed to be, so Nick could share just what he was supposed to share with me. It's like that for Indians—we who are right where we are supposed to be.

6

A Seed Is Planted

THE MADISON INDIAN COMMUNITY met every Sunday at the Wil-Mar Neighborhood Center on the east side of town. Indian families whose children were in the Madison city schools, Indian students who were attending the university, and Indians who lived in or near Madison came together every Sunday for a potluck meal, drumming, and most of all, visiting. I began to attend.

At my first meeting, I saw a handsome Indian man standing on the small stage in the community room. My friend said, "That's John Beaudin." He was asking everyone to donate used books he could take to the library on the Lac Courte Oreilles (LCO) Ojibwe Reservation in northern Wisconsin. I had to concentrate to keep from staring. John's eyes were sparkly blue with that little-boy devilishness in them that drew everyone to him.

He was an attorney and a respected leader in the Madison Indian community and in the larger Wisconsin Indian community. Still young, he carried in him the wisdom and visions of an elder. In 1992, he became LCO's chief tribal judge.

Each week that I attended the Wil-Mar, I talked with John more. After he heard my story, he always made me tell it to

John Beaudin was featured on the cover of the UW–Madison alumni magazine in 1992.

newcomers. It was a long story of how I always knew I was adopted and how hard it was to live as I had in an all-white town, the only Indian girl. His eyes always lit up when I got to the part about looking for and finding my family.

John had already battled and won against cancer when we met—a cancer he probably contracted from chemical exposure while serving in Vietnam. His great sense of humor mixed with his intelligence drew in people from all walks of life. He never seemed to distinguish between rich or poor, educated or uneducated. He was always teaching, and he loved to powwow dance. He respected any conversation that was extended his way and demonstrated to us all that everyone had something to offer. John always wanted to make sure everyone felt welcome, and he taught me how to extend myself to newcomers, how to walk up to them, shake their hands, and say hello. Most of all, he always offered his encouragement to anyone who seemed to need it.

He encouraged me, too.

Over the next year, I began to make many friends in the Indian community. I was still not able to work, so I had time to attend many of the functions that took place on the University of Wisconsin–Madison campus. One beautiful fall day, a few of us were sitting in Memorial Union, which is right on the shore of Lake Mendota, with its large windows looking out to the lake. This lovely setting was a common gathering spot for Native students during the day. In conversation, John mentioned that he was scheduled to speak at Edgewood College soon, but that something had come up and he could not keep his commitment. He turned to me and said, "Sandy, you should go in my place."

I thought he was teasing. Like, sure, *I* should go and talk? I just met my Indian family three years ago. I was still trying not to stare at the beautiful brown faces of the Indians I was meeting, still needing to fill the huge void created by decades of separation. What would I have to share with a classroom of college kids studying Indian history?

Convinced he was teasing, I continued to smile and didn't respond. He said, "Well? You should." I could feel the fear, shame, and hurt begin to rise out of my heart. He again said, "You can do it, Sandy."

I couldn't find any words other than, "What would I talk about?"

He said, "Tell them your story. They need to hear about these kinds of things."

I knew that when John said you should do something, people took him seriously. Besides, I had heard that if you are asked to do something, the person asking must see something in you that tells them you are the person for the task. Even if you feel you cannot do it well, you should do it to the best of your ability. But I was just not as convinced as he was that I was ready for this.

I took a deep breath, and we talked. The next thing I knew, I was on the phone with the professor at Edgewood College, confirming the date to speak to her class.

I had so much anxiety. What am I going to say? What do I bring to the class to show them? I brought books that I liked. I brought sage and I burned some, because I was afraid and sage helped me through fear.

I began by saying, "My name is Sandy White Hawk. I was born on the Rosebud Reservation in South Dakota. I did not get to grow up there, because I was adopted by white missionaries and raised here in Wisconsin." Then I surprised myself by saying, "When you meet most Indians, they can tell you where they come from and who they are related to and how their family came to live where they live. I can't tell you any of that, because I was taken from my family. I have to try to put it back together now. I am thirty-seven years old, I have never fit in anywhere, and only now is my life making sense."

The students listened intently as I told my story through the memories of my childhood. Afterward, the room was filled with emotion, and students wanted to know more. They said, "You need to write a book—this story would make a great movie."

When I told John the good news, he smiled and said, "They call me every year. You should do it from now on." And I did. For five years I told my story to the students at Edgewood College. Each year my confidence grew as the shame and humiliation of my story diminished.

I had been to several community feasts and always loved eating fry bread. Some variation of fry bread is found on most reservations. It was originally made from government rations of lard and flour, back when the reservations were first formed. Just as the African American community has soul food, much of which is made from parts of the animals their white enslavers threw away, Native Americans have food made from the rations given to them.

Fry bread is made either with or without yeast. When made correctly, it is delicious. I say *correctly* because it is an art. Not everyone can make good fry bread. A good fry bread maker is vital for any feast. It is usually a woman, but some men are great fry bread makers as well.

I decided I wanted to learn to make fry bread. After I made a few batches, I invited several people over for fry bread and chili. John broke off a piece of bread, chewed slowly, and said, "You could use just a little more sugar." Then we all began to visit and tell stories, and we ate the fry bread that needed a little more sugar. Just because it needed a little more sugar did not make it inedible. It was still fry bread.

I was sitting next to John on a stool with my knees drawn up close to my chest. Suddenly I realized I was wearing shorts— I had forgotten to change into pants. I have awful scars on my inner thighs. When I was fourteen, an M-80 firecracker accident left me with huge, long scars and pockets where tissue that had been blown out never grew back. I was very self-conscious about them. I had been teased about them, and I had dealt with the twisted faces of those who stared and slowly asked me, as if they were in pain, "What happened to your legs?"

I got up from the table to get something, and when I came

back John happened to look over and see my scars. He said, "What happened to your legs?" Everyone stopped talking and looked at me. My face burned red. I rarely told the story. I suffered years of post-traumatic stress disorder (PSTD) caused by the huge blast. Even twenty-three years later, I still did not feel comfortable revisiting the details. But John had asked.

I was riding in the back seat of a car with some boys. One sitting in front lit and threw an M-80 out the window. His hand bumped the top of the opened window, knocking the M-80 out of his hand and into the back seat. It landed in my lap. The explosion was devastating to my ears and my body. I was fortunate that I had several coats and a large portable radio in my lap, which helped contain the blow. The force of the M-80 blew away flesh from deep within my thighs. The boys took me to the emergency room, where the doctors had to carefully remove pieces of the radio that were embedded in my flesh. The doctors told my mother that they were just waiting for my exposed main artery to burst. I spent weeks in the hospital recuperating, but it was not my time to go.

By the time I was done with all the details, my heart was racing, as it always did when I relived that trauma.

The others at the table said things like, "Wow, Sandy, that's horrible."

John, chewing slowly, looked at me thoughtfully and said, "Well, what I wonder is, can your legs pick up WOJB today?"

WOJB is the radio station on the Lac Courte Oreille Ojibwe Reservation in northern Wisconsin. And we all laughed hard.

This interaction was so huge for me. I had never had laughter in the place of this pain. No one had ever seen my scars without making some negative look or comment, even if they did not mean to. It is a true art to be able to tease appropriately in a situation like that, and when it happens, it is healing.

There were many times when I wanted to live closer to South Dakota, closer to my brother and his family. I wanted to know more about what it meant to be from Rosebud. I love the feeling of the land beneath my feet, the open sky. I would get lonely. John told me not to worry that I lived so far from the reservation where I was born. He said that the Indian people in Madison were my neighbors, and just like when you're making a cake and you're out of sugar, you ask your neighbor if you can borrow some sugar. He gives it to you, and when you can, you pay it back.

It's like that for us as Indian people, he said. There are things most Indians share in understanding: sweats, and the uses of tobacco, sage, cedar, and sweetgrass, to mention a few. The rest—your Indian name, the kids' Indian names, and other ceremonies—will come in time, in your language. But, for now, you can borrow what you need from us, your neighbors.

I was with John and a few others from the Indian community at Senator Russ Feingold's victory party in 1992, enjoying the festivities. John turned to me and said, "You are going to do well. I am really proud of you. You did not go after ceremony to make you Indian. You have learned being Indian is about community. You'll find the ceremonies when it is time. You are going to do well."

We hoped it wouldn't happen, but it did. In 1993, John got sick again. This time it was obvious that he was on his way home. Janice, his wife, had used all her time off from work and needed help. We all decided to pitch in and help the hospice team.

I took my time with John, filling in two-hour intervals. Sometimes we visited. Other times I sat in silence as he slept.

On one of my visits, I took John to the hospital for one of his transfusions. We sat in the clinic waiting room with the other patients, everyone looking tired and weak. The wheelchair looked huge compared to John's now thin, frail frame. He sat hunched over with his elbows resting on the arms, holding his weight, his hands clasped together as if to lock in his balance. He kept his head down and spoke through his pain. "How was that conference you just went to?" I told him about the volunteer recruitment training conference I had just attended in Washington, DC. He always wanted to know details: what was said, what you learned, and most importantly, what are you going to do with what you learned.

Then he said, "You know, you should put a conference of adoptees together. You all have a lot to talk about." I stared at my feet, feeling unsure. It was like the time he told me I should talk to a college class. We didn't say any more about it, but the seed was planted.

A week later, I sat on the couch in the living room, a few feet from his hospital bed. He was weak, but as always, he loved to visit. I was hoping he would be awake for my time with him, because I wanted to tell him my latest news. "John, guess what?" I began. "I found another sister."

"Really?" he said, and with his shaky strength began to lift himself to sit up in the bed. "Tell me the whole story."

I began my story, "Well, my sister-in-law called last night and had my sister on the phone at the same time, and . . ."

"No," he interrupted, "I mean from the beginning."

"You mean from the beginning of how I always knew I was adopted and how I made it home the first time?" I asked unbelievingly.

He smiled and said, "Yes, from the beginning."

So I did. I started with my whole story from the beginning. A story he had heard over and over, a story he encouraged me to tell others over and over again, so much that we used to laugh each time John would have me tell my story. He never wanted to hear the short version!

John smiled, and his tired eyes got a sparkle as he waited for all the details he'd grown accustomed to hearing. When I got to the part about the recent phone meeting with my sister, he listened so closely. He laughed when I said, "My sister-in-law was laughing at how much we sounded alike on the phone."

John said, "Really, what else did you talk about? Where did she grow up and how did she find you?"

I finished the story just in time for the next hospice care worker to come. I walked over to his bed, gave him a hug, put on my leather coat, and said, "I won't see you for two weeks. I'm going to Florida for vacation."

He said, "Okay, give me a hug."

"I already hugged you, John—without my coat, because my coat will be cold on you."

"Just hug me with your ol' dead cow, aye!" he laughed.

I hugged him again and said, "See you in two weeks" as I walked out the door.

It was our last visit. John passed while I was in Florida. I missed his funeral. I was, however, able to be there for his memorial service. People of every color were there—Hispanic, Hmong, Black, and white. I learned more about John Beaudin, the lawyer who helped so many through his practice. I learned about John Beaudin, the friend who encouraged so many, young and old. And now I get to tell my John Beaudin stories.

John gave me a great gift by encouraging me to tell my own story over and over. The repetition removed the shame I felt about not knowing my culture, heritage, and identity. It normalized my life. The more I told my story, the more I learned, the more I understood. He taught me that I had something to share from the experience I had before I began to understand who I was as an Indian woman. It lit the passion in me to do the work I am doing today. That passion grew from the seed he planted during the discussion in the clinic waiting room.

7

The Seed Is Nurtured

HEALING DOES NOT HAVE A TIMELINE, and it comes in unexpected ways, through the ordinary activities of the day.

By 1991, I had been sober for eleven years and attended 12-step meetings regularly. My Menominee friend and I heard that there were Indian 12-step meetings in Black River Falls, the administrative center of the Ho-Chunk Nation, about two hours from Madison. So we drove there with great anticipation to sit with other sober Indians.

I sat listening to all those who shared before me. I was taking in all the brown faces in the room, still excited to be in a room full of Indians. But this was different. Being with only Indians was new, but being in recovery was not. I listened as they shared on the topic of the meeting, enjoying an inspiration that comes only from hearing how other addicts resolve their life's circumstances through a relationship with a higher power.

When it came my turn to talk, I was not even sure what prompted me to begin to say, "I've never been around this many Indians. It feels good but . . ." Overcome with sadness, I hung my head and began to cry. I rarely cried in front of anyone. I gathered myself enough to say I was adopted out and that being raised away from Indian people was terribly lonely and hard.

My face felt hot, a few tears fell into my lap, and my body tensed, resisting the relief of tears that pushed into my tear ducts. I was afraid that if I let myself feel this, I would not come back. And it was embarrassing to be so vulnerable in front of people I did not know.

A voice from the corner of the room said, "Someone sage her off." I sheepishly looked up to see someone kindly holding a shell of burning sage in front of me, gently pushing the floating smoke onto me.

Then the voice from the corner said, "Sister, what you are experiencing is grief. I am going to sing a song." His strong voice lifted into the air. I was deeply embarrassed to have caused such a commotion, to have stopped a meeting and have all the attention on me.

But as I listened to the song, the calming sage filling my nostrils and easing my soul, I felt the presence of an Eagle. She swooped into the room, came over to me, and put her wings around me in a hug. I doubted this reality and shamed myself into believing that I was making things up so I could really be Indian, whatever that meant.

But the woman from the Eagle nation stayed, regardless of my doubting her sacred presence. She stayed until just before the song was over. When the song ended, the man who sang said, "I am a Lakota traveling through and found this meeting. The song I sang for you was for your grief. The words in the song talk about how our relative the Eagle can take our grief away. We can put it on her wings and she can take it away."

I sat dumbfounded, now ashamed for *doubting* the healing experience. I said nothing and was so grateful that when this was all done the meeting continued as if this was a normal, everyday experience. When the meeting was over, I got lots of smiles, handshakes, and reaffirming hugs.

Grief. That's what that heaviness in my heart was, that heaviness that nearly took my breath away. It had a name, and I was learning about our ways to heal it through songs and ceremonies and the support of our communities. For when one hurts, we all hurt, because we are all related. I didn't know it at the time, but it taught me the healing power of our songs. That song nurtured the seed John had planted.

In the mid-1990s, a small Indian center opened on the east side of Madison. The center had secured a grant to support Indian people who wanted to test for their GED. Because Madison Area Technical College (MATC) offered tutoring to help people prepare for the exam, the center recruited volunteers to drive students across town to participate.

It was 1994, and I was finally feeling a little stronger. I was still weak and still had that horrible cognitive fog, but when I felt good, I volunteered as a driver. I enjoyed this immensely. I had earned an associate's degree at MATC in 1986, and the MATC Learning Center helped me catch up on my academics and prepare for college-level courses. I knew the staff would be very welcoming and helpful.

As I drove the students, I told them how I came to college without the ability to even write a complete sentence— because I didn't know what one was. In high school, I had been placed in a remedial reading class and saw a one-on-one tutor weekly. Mrs. Bauer was very nice, but no one seemed to notice how much I actually *read*. Any time I could, I went to the library and read, because I found some solace in reading. It didn't occur to me until I got into classes at MATC that I could read just fine. I just didn't retain the rules and vocabulary of English grammar; therefore, I failed English.

Part of the reason I wasn't retaining and learning was the complex trauma I was dealing with. I was in therapy for the PTSD from the firecracker accident. I had no idea who I was, no sense of belonging. Add to that the abuse at home. No one knew this about me. I was the best actress ever. My head was so full of trauma, and it took so much energy to hide it, there was no room for learning. I barely graduated. On senior skip day, I and others in my same situation had to go to detention all day while our classmates planned picnics and went swimming. I laughed and thought, *Oh, big deal.* I had already skipped so much school that it was a routine, no longer exciting. So I sat in that room all day, reading something. On graduation day 1971, I walked across the stage feeling like a fraud.

In the fall of 1971, I enrolled at MATC, and they gave us a placement test. I stared at the familiar format: multiple-choice questions with little circles next to answers. I didn't even read the questions, as I knew I wouldn't know the answers anyway. I did what I always did. I made a pattern, filling in the dots. One of the room proctors must have seen this and asked me to come with her. I thought, *How am I in trouble? I haven't even looked around the room to try to cheat. I didn't even talk to anyone.*

When we got into the other room, she put a blank sheet of paper in front of me and instructed me to write a complete sentence. I thought, *What? Damn it, I don't know what that means.* But then I remembered a teacher in high school once said that the shortest sentence in the Bible was "Jesus wept." So I wrote, "Jesus wept." Then she said, "Write another one." I was stuck. I felt really stupid, but she was nice to me. She said that based on my transcripts, I would need to go to the Learning Center for tutoring, and she enrolled me in all the classes I needed to be prepared for college classes. I basically retook high school classes, but this time I learned. I eventually caught up, and in the first semester of "real" college classes, I shocked myself when I made the dean's list.

By the time I was telling this part of the story to the student I was driving, we would be pulling into the MATC parking lot and the student would be wide-eyed with hope that maybe they too would pass their classes. When I saw MATC now had a Minority Student Services office, I took the students in and introduced them to the Native American student advisor, so they would have assistance navigating through the system.

One day while I was waiting for a student who was talking with the Native American advisor, the director of the office stepped out from her corner cubical. She introduced herself and asked me who I was. I told her my name and that I was a volunteer for this program assisting Indian students to get their GED and then enroll at MATC. She literally looked me up and down, and then said, "There will be an opening for the Native American student advisor. You should apply for it."

I was shocked, standing there in old sweats with my hair just loosely pulled back. "I'm on disability for chronic fatigue syndrome. I couldn't commit to the hours."

She surprised me by offering, "You could start part-time as an emergency hire for six months. Then we can reevaluate." My ears were ringing; my mouth got dry. This was an exciting offer. I had such a good experience at MATC that I'd love to encourage students through their years there.

I took the challenge. I became the Native American student advisor in 1994 and eventually worked full-time until 2000. It was basically my first job since being in the service, eighteen years earlier. All I knew was how to type. I grew so much during that time—I learned so much from the students. Eventually I learned how to organize an entire month of events dedicated to educating the Madison community about who Indians were. April was American Indian Month. I recruited speakers and organized a powwow, the Native American Student Association hosted Indian taco sales, and I learned I had skills I had never suspected.

Sometimes I was depressed and just wanted to be alone. I was recovering from all the abuse and isolation I went through growing up; healing from an emotionally abusive marriage of thirteen years; and coming to terms with this strange illness that left me weak and in pain. It was hard to believe that I had a real future, when all I could see was the past and my difficult present. Processing all of this at once left me exhausted, and sometimes I felt hopeless. As often as I would begin to feel that way and I would want to isolate, my friend would say, "Let's go to a powwow."

"I don't feel like it," I would moan. "I just want to stay home." I was experiencing feelings that I had not felt before, the feelings that I had first drowned with alcohol and then just learned to keep down.

Except now my usual method of pushing down the pain, sadness, and anger had worn out. Now these wounds were exposed to the light of the drum and songs. After some time, I realized that after being at a powwow, I felt better. I felt stronger. The healing and encouragement that happens during a powwow isn't visible, but it is real.

I began going to powwows any chance I got. I loved the sound of the drum, the beautiful, strong voices of the singers—everything about it. Powwow season begins in the spring, and in some regions of the country there are powwows almost every weekend. People can go from one to another on what is called "the powwow trail." I mostly went to the smaller traditional powwows. What I found most healing about these events was the visiting. I spent hours talking with those I saw regularly. Wearing the shawl my aunt Cecilia gave me, I danced intertribals—the dances where all who are there, whether they have an outfit or not, are welcome to join. When the subject came up, I told part of my story. But mostly I enjoyed not having to tell my story. I could just be me, coming into myself.

Ever since I saw my first powwow in 1989, I knew I wanted to dance, but I was afraid and mostly felt that I was not *Indian enough* to dance. After a few years, people started asking, "When you gonna get an outfit?" I would just smile and store the comment in that place where I keep things I don't know what to do with right away.

In 1997, I finally decided to make my first traditional outfit. I had used a sewing machine only in my high school home economics class in 1969. But with the help of Linda Metoxen, I designed and sewed my first traditional powwow outfit.

I had to walk through a lot of fear and anxiety again. By this time, my hair was waist-length—no longer "almost long enough for braids." I could braid it when I wore my powwow outfit.

Beginning to powwow dance is called "coming into the circle." The protocol calls for the dancer to choose the powwow, and I chose the small annual veterans' powwow hosted by the University of Wisconsin Indigenous Law Student Association. The dancer has a giveaway: you place items on a blanket that are given to someone whom you have selected ahead of the event, someone who has supported you, and then additional gifts for others—usually elders, veterans, drummers, singers, and dancers. This shows your appreciation for the people who make up the circle you are about to join.

Gift giving is a regular practice among all Indian tribes. For a new dancer, it is a way to show generosity and acknowledge those who will now support you as you begin to be part of community—part of "the powwow circle."

In 1998, I was honored by being asked to be head woman veteran dancer at the Highground Pow Wow, a veterans' powwow held at a park near Neillsville, Wisconsin. It started at 7:00 PM on Friday and went to about 5:00 PM on Sunday. I started dancing Friday and was mostly on my feet dancing through Saturday. By Sunday morning I was moving very slowly. My body was carrying residual CFS symptoms of muscle pain, fatigue, and heaviness. *Come on*, I coaxed myself into trying to get my hair braided quickly with my cramping, tired fingers, but it was not enough. I was going to be late.

I drove to the powwow grounds feeling a little guilty but thinking that all I would get was a good teasing about being late. I parked my car and caught a ride in the rented golf cart the powwow committee used to transport those of us who needed help with the long walk down the hill and over to the powwow arena. The driver dropped me off close to the arena, and I walked over as quickly as I could in my outfit and moccasins.

The powwow committee had already begun their giveaway. As I made my way to the arena, I heard my name called over the loudspeaker once, then a pause, and then they called me once again. As I approached the circle, the MC laughed and said, "Ah, here she is," and waited for me to make my way into the circle and over to the MC stand.

I shook his hand, took my gift, and began moving down the

line of people who had received their gifts, shaking everyone's hand. The line formed a circle, and when I shook the last person's hand, I turned to stand next to him, waiting for the next person to do the same. I was standing next to Trudell Gareau. I had met him and others of the 173rd Airborne Brigade Color Guard the day before. They were the invited color guard from Minneapolis. Trudell was from Rosebud and was now living with his family in St. Paul, Minnesota. I rarely met another Lakota in Wisconsin, let alone someone from Rosebud. I was so happy to see someone from my homeland.

We shook hands, smiled, and chatted as we watched the others receive their gifts. He asked if I was going to Rosebud Fair. I said, "Yes, I love going home whenever I can."

He said, "Good." He then began to tell me what it was like for him to grow up on the reservation. We are about the same age, so what he was describing of the reservation is what I could have experienced. When he was a child, Trudell's family went to Rosebud Fair every year in a horse-drawn wagon, and they camped out for the four days of the fair. His eyes were bright as he said that he loved that time on the reservation, that it was a special time. Then there was silence.

I was happy for the pictures he painted for me. Something to fill the landscape of what it used to be like, or what it could have been for me if I grew up there.

He turned to me and said, "I'm sorry you missed all that." He said it so sincerely, without dramatization. It was a pure, genuine acknowledgment of my loss. And then he turned back to shake the hand of another person coming through the line.

My mind was in shock; my heart beat with excitement. I know he had no idea what it meant to me to hear those unexpected, healing words. No one had addressed my loss or pain so directly. It had been unspoken, carried through a look or gesture. But he said the words out loud: "I'm sorry you missed all that." And this gift of compassion came from a Lakota relative, which made it more meaningful.

I thanked him and continued to shake the hands of those

who came through the line, not wanting to be overly emotional. We didn't talk much after that. It didn't matter. Those six words lifted years of heavy separation off my spirit.

It was August 1999 and I was at Rosebud Fair, our tribe's annual powwow. When I first met my family, they told me I should come to Rosebud Fair because I could meet relatives who come home to visit. Annual powwows are like that across Indian Country. All who can make it come to visit family and friends and make new friends. At every annual powwow, there are also adoptees who are looking for relatives. I had started bringing my children, so they could get to know my brother Leonard's kids, their cousins, who had also visited us in Wisconsin.

I learned that Leonard worked at the Antelope Senior Center in Mission. When I went to Rosebud, I would try to visit him at work, because often I'd get to meet some of the elders living there. It was there that I met Clara, one of the residents. We became instant friends. She told me how much she liked my brother. One of the things she liked most was that he could speak Lakota.

As I walked around the powwow looking for a place to sit, I spotted Clara. She waved me to the empty seat next to her. As we watched the dancing, she told me stories of when she was young. The afternoon session was coming to a close. It was that time of day when the sun sets and is so beautiful, especially at the powwow grounds. The whole arena reflects the last golden hues, and for a while it seems we are transported back to days of our ancestors, before the pain and shame of colonization. The powwow announcer said there was going to be "a special" before the supper break. At a special, a person or family acknowledges someone or some event with an honor song and a giveaway.

The family's spokesperson stood in front of the announcer's stand and began to introduce the elder Korean War veteran they were honoring. The family assembled baskets of giveaway items and placed them in front of the announcer's stand. This giveaway was a way of thanking the veterans for their service and for attending the powwow. The drum began singing the honor song.

The family began to enter the arena, walking to the slow beat of the drum, the honored elder leading the way. After they made one complete walk around the arena, the announcer invited all veterans to come out and dance with the family. Clara nudged my arm and said, "Get out there: you're a veteran."

I said, "Yes, I just want to watch a minute." I was struck by this elder Indian woman, wrapped in a shawl, stepping gracefully to the beat of the drum. When the honor beats were hit, she and the others raised their hands, looking off in the distance. She looked so beautiful in the setting sunlight.

Honor songs are done a little differently in the various regions of Indian country. In the Plains, an honor song begins with a slow beat, and everyone walks slowly. The beat stays steadily slow, and then honor beats are hit—three strong, hard beats. This is when all the dancers raise and hold one hand in the air. Those who carry eagle fans raise them at this time. They walk around until the drumbeat picks up to the rhythm of a round dance. In the round dance, people stand shoulder to shoulder, facing the center of the circle and stepping to the distinctive round dance beat. Everyone is invited to join, the energy picks up, and everyone begins to smile.

As I was watching everyone in the arena, I started asking Clara questions. I wanted to know the words to the veteran's song that was being sung in Lakota. She said the song was saying, "Thank you for what you have done for us." I told her that I had come into the powwow circle in Wisconsin and had not really seen a Lakota honor song before. I knew that it was very rude to be pesky with one question after another, but I was compelled, and I had to ask.

"Why do they raise their hands at the honor beats?"

She said, "Right now they are acknowledging all those veterans who went into service and gave their lives in service. They are saying, 'Thank you for giving your lives so that we may live.'" The song continued, and more veterans came out to the arena, first shaking the honored elder's hand and then the family's hands and falling into place at the end of the line. There was another group of honor beats, and Clara explained, "Now they are acknowledging all those veterans who are in service right now. They are saying, 'Thank you for your service. We're glad you are here; welcome home.'"

That's when it hit me.

We have songs for everything. I have heard honor songs sung for someone's sobriety, at a naming, for graduating. We can even ask someone to make a song for a special. But I had never seen a song to welcome adoptees home.

I finally got up and went out to finish the dance. My mind was racing. What if, at every annual powwow, the announcer would say, "At this time, we are going to acknowledge our relatives who were separated from us through adoption and foster care and have made their way back to us. If you are an adoptee or someone who grew up in foster care, please come out to the middle so we can acknowledge you. You adoptees, this song is for you, we are glad you're here, and we welcome you home." And what if we took it even further and said, "Those of you who have a relative out there, and you are waiting for them to return, join us. We'll all dance together for their return."

I returned to Clara, keeping my thoughts to myself. Then I realized that I was sitting in the same bleachers where I sat ten years earlier, in 1989, when I attended my first powwow in Rosebud on my second trip home. It was the first time I heard the drum and saw our traditional outfits. I had been overwhelmed with the strength, the beauty. I had so wanted to be a part of it. But I didn't feel I was part of the circle. I watched the dancers walk in and out of the circle. I watched the children laughing, running in and out of the circle. I saw the intertribal dances, when I could dance even without an outfit. But I did not. I felt that I was not worthy, not Indian enough.

In those ten years, I had healed many wounds caused by separation from my family and culture. Much of my healing took place through songs and ceremonies. I also knew there were other adoptees at the powwow feeling the same way I did in the beginning, like an outsider, not Indian enough.

I wanted other adoptees to feel good about themselves. I wanted them to feel part of the circle, and I knew a song would help. But then, *what did I know?* I had only come into myself recently. I took these thoughts and tucked them away in the place full of things that I am not sure what to do with, but know I should not throw away.

In 2000, I was still working at Madison Area Technical College, and I had invited Chris Leith to be one of our speakers during American Indian Month in April. I had met Chris the summer before, when I was invited to go to World Peace and Prayer Day in Costa Rica.

Chris was a highly respected First Nations Dakota spiritual leader and Korean War air force veteran from the Prairie Island Reservation in Minnesota. I was impressed by his many gifts and talents. But what impressed me more than anything was how he led us in prayer. He said, "I am going to pray in my Dakota language, the language given to me at birth. Pray along with me in your own language. Pray from your heart, not your head. Your heart has more wisdom than your head ever will." That struck me, and I was excited to bring this man to campus for our students.

The morning of his presentation, I met him for breakfast. We were catching up from our first meeting in Costa Rica. I must have really felt relaxed, as I found myself telling him about my experience in Rosebud the previous August. I told him everything I was thinking. What if we did a song for our adoptee relatives? It would help the healing. We have songs for everything, but no song for our returning relatives. When I finished explaining, I was overcome with fear. I wished I could take it all back, because I should not have been talking like this to an elder. Who am I? What do I know?

Chris stopped eating, put his fork down, and said, "You're right. There should be a song for adoptees. I'll get Jerry Dearly to make a song, and we'll bring it out to the people at World

Chris Leith, early 2000s

Peace and Prayer in June." He told me that he was on the board of the National Indian Child Welfare Association and that this is what the Indian Child Welfare Act was about, bringing back the extended family. "The NICWA conference is in Tucson next month. You should try to get there. That would be a good place to get the word out that we'll be bringing the song out for the first time."

Then he said, "You better give me some tobacco, my girl. You've had a vision."

I laughed nervously and said, "I always thought you had to be on a hill or fasting to have a vision."

He laughed, too, and said, "The Creator can give us a vision anywhere when our heart is ready."

As we walked to our cars to drive to the college, I told him about my job duties and the joy I found in working with the students. He very casually said, "I think you have found your purpose in life"—and he was clearly talking about my ideas for helping adoptees.

I didn't say anything, mostly out of respect. He was an elder telling me something important. But I had this great job that I loved. After all my struggles, I had a great wage, benefits, and retirement. Why would I leave that—and to do what? It was also hard because—as sometimes happened—his words seemed to be too good to be about me. What did I know? Who did I think I was? But his words stayed in my heart: "purpose in life." I had literally never heard that phrase before, and I never would have thought of it pertaining to me. What would it mean if helping adoptees was my purpose in life? I thought about it for five minutes and then stuck it in that drawer, another thing I didn't know what to do with.

But I did decide to go to Tucson.

The National Indian Child Welfare Association evolved in the 1980s to become the country's leading organization working to support the safety, health, well-being, and spiritual strength of American Indian/Alaska Native children. The next week I applied for travel funds to go to their conference, pointing out that several of my students were adoptees or had been in foster care. The funding was approved, but the college travel budget was small, so in order to pay my fees for registration and an informational table, I also served as a conference volunteer.

I reported to the NICWA registration table and said, "Put me to work." My first job was to help fold NICWA T-shirts for the sales table. It was fun to get to know the NICWA staff and talk with the conference participants. After a few hours, I was released to attend some of the workshops.

I checked my table, where I had placed copies of a one-page statement and a flyer announcing that the song for adoptees would be sung for the first time at World Peace and Prayer Day in the Black Hills, South Dakota. I saw that quite a few flyers had been taken, which pleased me greatly. "At least there is interest," I thought to myself.

The next day I showed up at the registration table to see how I could help. They needed someone to transport elders. The main conference hotel was at the bottom of a steep walkway, and the conference workshops were at the top. I would be driving a golf cart, shuttling elders up and down the wide, paved walkway. I brought flyers with me to pass out to my passengers, and I had a great time visiting with Indians from all over the country during the short ride. One beautiful, round gramma insisted on giving me a two-dollar tip.

After one of my deliveries, I reached the bottom of the hill and found one middle-aged Indian man. He was dressed in jeans and cowboy boots and had long, shiny black hair that he wore in a ponytail. Since no one else was around, I asked him, "Do you want a ride?"

He looked around and said, "sure," and hopped into the cart. He looked down at my snakeskin cowboy boots and said, "I like your boots."

I smiled and said, "Thank you. I skinned these snakes myself. One bit me so I had to kill it. Then I killed his brother, too!" We laughed even harder when I told him that I had convinced this white girl that I had really done that. He had a nice smile, and I liked the sound of his voice. I dropped off the handsome Indian man and didn't think anything more about him. The Creator had a plan, though, that both of us were unaware of. This man, George McCauley, became my husband. But that is another story.

The local Indian community sponsoring the NICWA conference had a powwow in the evening, and I brought my powwow outfit so I could dance. At one point Chris said it was time to make the announcement about the song. We walked over to the announcer's stand, and the announcer handed Chris the microphone. Chris talked about how he had been brought on to the NICWA board as a grassroots elder. His message was the importance of healing the extended family. He said one of the ways to do that was to bring home our relatives who had been adopted out. He then introduced me and handed me the microphone.

He had not told me that I was going to speak.

I was intimidated. Chris was such an eloquent speaker. He had just quieted a few hundred people with the tone of his voice and the message of hope of healing our families. And now I was supposed to speak, to follow him? Hoping that I hid my fear, I briefly shared my story and my thoughts about how a song could help those of us coming home—and help our communities to heal.

It was almost an out-of-body experience. I kept thinking, *Who do you think you are? You don't know anything. You don't even speak the language.* But I also thought about what I saw back at Rosebud Fair during the special for the Korean War veteran, and I tried to describe it as best I could. When we were done, several people came up to talk to me about their relatives who had been in foster care or adopted out and were still missing. I was surprised again that people were responding with such interest and encouragement.

After the conference, I went back to Madison, back to my job as a student advisor, happy that we got the word out but certainly not prepared for all that was about to unfold.

8

The Song

WORLD PEACE AND PRAYER DAY is the vision of Arvol Looking Horse, the Nineteenth-Generation Keeper of the Sacred White Buffalo Pipe. His idea was to bring people of all races and all faiths together to pray for world peace and global healing on June 21, the summer solstice. World Peace and Prayer Days had been held at Gray Horn Butte, Wyoming (also known as Devils Tower); Joseph Bighead Reserve (Cree Nation), Canada; Pipestone Quarry, Minnesota; and in Costa Rica. In 2000, the Wopila (Thank You) Ceremony was held in the Black Hills to give thanks for the gift of these four events that brought many Indigenous people together to pray for world peace and healing of our Mother Earth.

Paha Sapa (the Black Hills) are sacred to the Lakota and known as the "the heart of everything that is." The spiritual significance of all of this—my journey home to Rosebud, meeting Chris Leith and the other spiritual leaders, now about to hear a song for adoptees, the very thing I had been envisioning—was overwhelming. All I could do was move slowly and try to take it all in. This sacred place was where the song was going to be sung for the first time. It was far beyond anything I had ever experienced or even dreamed.

I arrived in the evening of June 20, just as the sun was setting. I walked into the event wearing my jeans, hooded sweatshirt, and cowboy boots. It had rained earlier, and the evening air had that crisp, not-quite-summer bite. I joined a group of people sitting under a canopy and saw my two friends, Chris Leith and Dave Chief.

I had met Dave Chief at World Peace and Prayer Day in Costa Rica. He was a spiritual advisor for the event and a close friend of Arvol Looking Horse. While Dave was an elder, his heart was young, and he still had young-man eyes set on his brown, weathered face.

I was greeted with, "We wondered if you were going to make it." I smiled, a little embarrassed, because I thought that since the song was not going to be brought out until the twenty-first, why would I need to be here sooner?

It was then I realized that the event had been going on since June 18, and they wanted me to be part of it. I was still new to these kinds of spiritual gatherings, unsure about how to prepare and be present from beginning to end. They were gracious and never scolded me. The message was clear in their faces that I had missed something that would have been good for me. It was the last time I was so lackadaisical in getting to and participating in ceremonies.

Night came quickly after the sun dropped behind the trees. As darkness set in, we went to our cabin. I was so grateful for this luxury, as many others camped out in the frosty night.

Among the campers were two vans full of Canadian adoptees who had driven thirty hours to be part of World Peace and Prayer Day and to hear the song for adoptees. I was so surprised by this commitment and asked them how they found out about the song way up in Canada. The woman who brought them said she got a flyer while attending the NICWA conference in Tucson. There were many such happenings, as spirit led other adoptees to the events.

I went to sleep in the cozy cabin and awoke in the morning to the sun shining through the sheer curtain. I tried to roll over, to block out the light so I could sleep longer, but the birds were singing loudly, as if they were saying, "Come on. Today is the day! Get up!"

The birds' morning songs reminded me of Stella Pretty Sounding Flute, an elder I met in Costa Rica. Her niece Belinda Faye Jo traveled with her, as she needed assistance, and the three of us had shared a room. On June 21, 1999, Stella woke us up and said, "Get up girls! It's prayer day. The birds have been up a half hour already." We rolled out of bed, heads still heavy with sleep and embarrassed that this elder had way more energy than we did.

I sat up and looked out the window at a wide opening, at least as big as a football field, only circular and surrounded by dense trees. It was beautiful. The sun made the green greener; the sky was clear blue without a cloud to be seen. The bugs had already begun their morning songs, harmonizing with the birds. I gathered myself and began to get ready.

I was remembering what Dave Chief said about our traditional clothing. He told us to wear it to events, that it especially made the old people feel good. I brought my powwow outfit, but I was still self-conscious about wearing it. I asked Chris if I should, and he said yes, so I did. We ate breakfast, laughed, and visited, and then made our way over to where the people had circled up, ready to begin the day.

I don't recall all the blessings that other culture groups did, but I do remember being absolutely amazed at the similarities Indigenous cultures have in their relationship to Mother Earth.

Then I saw something that brought me to tears: a Horse Ceremony. The Lakota have a special relationship with horses. There are special songs and medicines for horses. In this ceremony, several riders came in from the east, as the drummers' voices rose to greet them. I saw the eyes of the horses, and it looked as if they knew what they were doing and understood the sacredness of this day. They lifted their feet just a little more elegantly to the beat of the drum and held their heads in a regal way, acknowledging the Creator and what we were doing. It was profound, and I cried tears of healing release.

Sometime after this, it was time for Chris and me to make

our presentation. I had no idea what was going to happen. We walked up to an opening in the circle. I scanned the circle and saw the few hundred people gathered. When Chris began to speak, his quiet voice once again silenced everyone. They listened intently. He talked about his work with the National Indian Child Welfare Association as a board member and their spiritual advisor. He talked about how our families need healing, and he said that we were going to do something today to begin healing those families who had been harmed by foster care and adoption. Then he said, "I am going to turn the microphone over to Sandy White Hawk, so she can tell her story and share her vision."

When Chris said, "and share her vision," I was again immediately intimidated, just as before. I did not want anyone to think that I thought I was "somebody." Sharing a vision just seemed like a thing someone else should be doing. But in that moment of self-doubt, I again thought about why I wanted a song, and remembering my feeling during the veteran's honor song at Rosebud Fair seemed to give me the courage to speak.

I began. "I was born on the Rosebud Reservation and adopted out to a white missionary family. My life was not easy." I told about the anger, fear, sadness, and isolation of being the only Indian girl in my hometown. I talked about how hard it was to make my way back to my family.

Then I shared the vision I saw at Rosebud Fair the previous year. I talked about this song being not just for adoptees, but for all those who are behind every adoptee: mothers, fathers, grandparents, aunts, uncles, brothers, sisters, cousins. When one is taken, it affects everyone in that family circle.

I said that I wanted a song, a song just for us, to encourage us. "I know that the sound of the drum can go into that place in our heart where words can't go; that the drum and the song can heal." I returned the microphone to Chris.

He then introduced Jerry Dearly, an Oglala Lakota from the Pine Ridge Reservation. He lives in St. Paul, Minnesota. Jerry is known for the gift of song-making. He is also an eyapaha—an announcer, a speaker for the people. He is asked to MC many powwows throughout the year because of his vast knowledge of the powwow way, traditional songs, and protocols.

About ten years before, I had seen his name on an old pow-wow tape of the Porcupine Singers. They were one of the premier drum groups in the 1970s. Now here I was, meeting him.

Jerry took the microphone, and in his strong, melodic announcer voice began to tell a little about himself. He talked

---

Song for the orphans! Completed, Tuesday, May 23, 2000, 12:48 AM

Wablenica ki blihic'iya po

Lakol wicoh'an ki anagoptan po wowaś'akelo

Hoka hoka he

Cancega ta ho ki nayah'un pelo

English translation:

(orphans) (the) (be strong) (many)
Wablenica ki blihic'iya po

(Lakota way tradition)(the) (listen to them)   (strength, they give you)
Lakol wicoh'an ki anagoptan po wowaś'akelo

(Energize, energize)
Hoka hoka he

(drum) (its)(voice)   (you hear it telling you things)
Cancega ta ho ki nayah'un pelo

A treasured photocopy of the Wablenica Song

about where he came from and his sobriety, and then he began talking about the song. "Chris called me and asked me to make a song for wablenica, orphans." He explained he had agreed to write the song, and then didn't think about it for a while. Later, Chris asked him if he had made it yet. "Working on it," Jerry told him. Chris called a few times before Jerry was inspired to make the song. "Then one afternoon, I heard a bird singing, and as I listened, it came to me."

My part of the talking was over, and I was starting to relax as I listened to Jerry speak. Then he said, "Sandy, go out and stand in the center." And again, the feelings of fear, anxiety, doubt flooded my body. *What? No way. This isn't what I wanted.* I breathed hard, trying to hide my emotions, but I must not have been successful, as my friend Jean Day came out and stood with me. I was grateful for her company.

Jerry continued the story of how he made this special honor song. He sang the Wablenica Song through once without the drum, and then walked over to the drum group. He had given the group a cassette copy of the song the day before so they could learn it. They began to sing. Their voices were strong, and the beat of the drum seemed to come up from the ground.

I walked to the outer edge of the inside of the circle to start the honor dance. I stepped to the slow stomp beat, looking down at my moccasins as they walked on this sacred site where our ancestors had walked and prayed before us. Then I recalled a dream I had twelve years earlier—before I had even heard a drum. I dreamt a slow beat, faint singing. I had told a friend about it, and both of us just wrote it off as one of those strange, unexplainable dreams you have.

But here I was hearing that same drum. My heart recognized it. I *knew* it. I heard the singers' voices rise above the beat, and my heart jumped. I thought I was going to fall to my knees. It was a release of what I had kept in for so long: a vision, a dream, a desire for a song to recognize and welcome adoptees, birth relatives home. The Creator had put it in my heart long before, and here it was. The release was overwhelming. I reached down and picked up a rock, wanting a piece of the earth that witnessed this sacred moment.

The announcer invited other adoptees to come into the circle, and we all began to walk to the slow beat, until it picked up to end in round dance. When the song was done, everyone was smiling and laughing, shaking hands. Joy was in the air. It was just as I envisioned: sharing the grief, releasing it in song, and then being given the joy of hope that our relatives will find their way back. And if they could not make it home, at least we acknowledged them.

As I walked back to my chair, I lost count of how many people came up to shake my hand and say thank you. I felt self-conscious, of course, and I kept thinking, *It's not me. I didn't make the song.*

Then a man about my age said to me with tears in his eyes, "Thank you for this. When I was little, social services wanted to take me and my sisters away from my mother. She got me and three older ones back to the reservation, but social services got my two youngest sisters, and they got adopted out. We found one but are still looking for the other. This is the first time I ever got to dance and pray for her like this. Thank you, thank you."

An elder woman came up to me and cupped my hand in her soft, wrinkled brown hands. She said, "Thank you for this song. Thank you for thinking of my grandson. The last time I saw him, he was in diapers. I think he is out in New York." She wiped a tear from her cheek and shook my hand again and then walked away.

It is one thing to know something in your head. It is another to see it unfold in the hearts of those whom you intended for it to help. I watched her walk away, stunned at what was unfolding. This was what I wanted. Now it was happening.

Just then, another woman said she had something for me. We walked to a quiet spot and sat down on the ground. She said that in Canada they had been working to find their adoptees. They had received money from the Canadian government for programs, but they did not have this, meaning a song and public acknowledgment and welcoming. She had placed a bundle between us and began opening it. A bundle is considered a precious personal medicine for empowerment of healing and spirituality. It can contain different items to be opened for specific occasions.

"I know this work is going to go to another level, and you are the one who is going to take it there," she told me. I could not think of what to say aloud, but in my head the words were loud and clear: *Tell her there is no "work." You just wanted a song, and here it is now, and anyone can take it and use it. It belongs to the people now.* And then I recalled the teaching: when someone asks you to do something, you should do it to the best of your ability. Ever since John Beaudin pushed me to do many things I did not think I could or should do, I had been trying to practice this when I was asked to speak or pray.

This woman was so sincere; I felt it would be too rude to say, *You got the wrong woman.* So I accepted the bundle, shook her hand, and thanked her.

I carried the bundle over to Chris and told him what happened. He just looked at me and said calmly, "Waste"— *wash-TAY*, good. I was trying to keep my mind open to what just happened. Now what was I supposed to do?

I was relieved that Chris thought the best way to finish the day was to sit in our lawn chairs and people watch. The sun was just beginning to start its descent. We joined the circle one more time for the closing ceremony of World Peace and Prayer Day 2000.

A few days later, I drove Chris to the Rapid City airport for his return flight. We sat outside in the warm sun until check-in time. He looked off into the distance and said, "The next time we bring the song out, we'll have to do a Wiping of Tears to heal the grief caused by the years of separation from family and culture."

I knew the Wiping of Tears Ceremony—it was done to help those who were grieving a death. But I thought to myself, *"The next time we bring the song out." What is he thinking?* Yet

Chris sat in the sun at the airport in Rapid City.

I was also moved. After he left, I sat in my car and wrote down some of our thoughts in a notebook.

I drove to Rosebud and stayed with my brother for a few days. When I got back to Madison, I invited several friends over for a meal and told them what happened in the Black Hills—the vision, the Wablenica Song, and how this bundle was given to me. Then, I tucked the bundle in my closet for the rest of the summer.

Soon after this, I was visiting with Davey Jean Okimosh at a powwow. She was a very well-respected Menominee elder who had befriended me. (I truly have never figured out why elders were so nice to me or liked to talk to me, but I sure have been blessed to call many my friends, and I have enjoyed their stories and learned from their lessons.)

Davey saw me and called me over to visit. She asked how I was and what I had been doing. I felt shy about describing my experience in the Black Hills, because I truly was not sure what it meant. I knew what I witnessed, but still, I wondered how I should talk about it. I can't recall what I said, but she asked the singers of the Junior Deadgrass Society, her family drum, to come and listen.

I told them how a busload of adoptees came from Canada. How this gramma came up to me and thanked me because she could now dance and pray for the grandchild she had not seen in many years.

The next thing I knew, I was starting to plan for the first Welcome Home Powwow for adoptees and formerly fostered relatives. It would happen on the Menominee Nation at Keshena, Wisconsin, in October 2001.

The powwow had to be approved by the Menominee Nation's Language and Culture Committee, which was mostly made up of elders. Chris had relationships with some Menominees, as he had been asked to run sweats for them. I also had very good friends on the Menominee Reservation. Still, I was uneasy about making such a big ask. As usual, I followed

Chris's lead. I was noticing how he respectfully nudged our people into providing space for healing.

We sat on a bench outside of the building, waiting for our turn to go before the committee. I looked up to see my journalist friend Patty Loew greeting us with her warm smile. She told me, "Sandy, I've been thinking about you. I found this rock in Lake Superior and thought of you, and I want you to have it." Rocks from the Great Lakes have spiritual significance. This one, though, was the shape of a mother wrapped in a blanket with a baby. How is that possible?

Patty didn't know about my deep feelings of inadequacy. If it were not for Chris, none of this would be happening. There I was, sitting in this inadequacy, fearing going before

Patty Loew's gift of this Mother Child Rock was a powerful reassurance.

the elders, and the Creator provides a sign to tell me that I am right where I am supposed to be. I held the rock and smiled at Patty, and we hugged.

The meeting was quiet and contemplative, with good questions, and it went by fast. The committee approved our request that the tribe sponsor the powwow.

It was the middle of August 2000. I was enjoying another summer powwow season, not yet deep in plans for the Welcome Home Powwow the next year. The phone rang, and I was happy to hear Chris Leith's voice. He told me about this traditional powwow called the Birch Coulee Gathering of Kinship at the Lower Sioux Indian Community in Morton, Minnesota. It was held in September. I remember his gentle voice said, "It'd be nice if you came for the powwow." We decided that we would bring the song out for any adoptees or fostered individuals at this gathering. I did not give it a lot of thought, as I was just following the lead of this elder.

The Gathering of Kinship took place near one of the battlefields in the war of 1862 between the Dakota and the United States. Chris and I drove there together in his Ford Expedition, listening to his country music and enjoying the beautiful fall weather. The site is far off the main road, not visible from the highway. The paved road ends, and a gravel road leads into a wooded area. We drove through the woods and then on to a clearing. All the while, I was thinking, *When I step onto the ground I may be stepping where some of my Dakota relatives not only walked, but lost their lives.* The powwow was small, yet there were two food stands and several craft stands. The energy in the air was relaxed and happy. We drove the truck through an area where no one but an elder and their assistant could drive. Chris parked the truck behind the announcer's stand.

A powwow announcer stand is usually a raised wooden stage that is fully covered. It's usually large enough for a few people to sit with the announcer at different times throughout the day, taking care of specials, raffles, and contests.

We went up to the announcer stand and found Jerry Dearly. He gave us a big smile and immediately we all started teasing each other. I looked around to find a good place to sit while Chris and Jerry conversed in Lakota.

I settled into my chair just a few feet from the announcer's stand, right behind a drum group, enjoying the sun and the great singing. A jingle dress dancer, a mother about my age, sat a couple of chairs down from me. We started speaking, and we were soon making jokes and laughing.

I noticed this handsome young man she was bringing drinks and food to. I asked her if he was her son, and she said "yes" with a proud mother's smile.

I said, "Hey, I got a daughter about his age," and we began to plan to become mothers-in-law. In the perfect September weather, this beautiful woodland setting that had been a battlefield was now a place of joy and healing.

I was enjoying the time visiting with my new friend when Chris leaned over and asked me, "Do you have an Indian name?"

"No," I replied.

"Well, you can't be doing this if you don't have an Indian name." I was not sure what he meant. *I can't be doing what?* I thought to myself.

Then he said, "You have a bundle now, and we are going to do this ceremony for the people. You have to have an Indian name."

Each tribe gives their members names in their own way. Indian names are kind of like baptismal names, given in ceremonies. It is understood that the spirits give you the name, and you use it to pray with. I always wanted a Lakota name but had not been around spiritual leaders until I met Chris and the other elders of the Seven Council Fires in Costa Rica.

Chris walked over to the announcer's stand and talked to Jerry, then came back, sat down, lit a cigarette, and said, "We'll do it in a little while." I sat there thinking, *But my children and friends are not here with me.* Then, just as quickly, I said to myself, *Have faith.*

About twenty minutes later, Jerry announced they were going to do a naming. The dance arena was cleared. Chris had me bring his buffalo skull and other sacred items out to the middle of the arena. He positioned me in front of the skull. Jerry waited for the signal to sing the pipe-filling song. Jerry led the full drum of about ten men. It was so beautiful. Then they sang the four directions song, another beautiful song that acknowledges the grandfathers in four directions. During this song, I felt the presence of an Eagle, as I had in the 12-step meeting years before. But again I doubted: *No way. Come on, Sandy. You just gotta see and hear stuff.* But it was so real. It was as if I could feel a female Eagle swoop down past me. I stood with my head down, praying, as they sang another prayer song. Chris prayed in Dakota with his pipe. He looked so strong and centered. He was dressed in his moccasins, a blue velvet breechcloth beaded with a floral design, a red ribbon shirt. On his head he wore his headdress. This great honor is reserved for chiefs and those who are recognized as earning the right to wear one. I helped Chris get ready for many ceremonies, and there was always something that overcame him once he had that on. Words are inadequate to describe.

The song was over, and Chris was just about done. The Eagle had left, and I felt like I was finally free from my crazy imagination. Jerry walked over to Chris, took the microphone, and began to speak. I will never forget what he said.

"A woman from the Eagle Nation flew here and saw Sandra's life: where she has been, where she is now, and where she is going to be in the future. She gave her the name Cokta Najiŋ Wiŋyaŋ, Stands in the Center Woman." I was shocked. And once again, I was embarrassed that when a spirit came to be with me, I thought it was my imagination. The drum sounded, and acknowledgments came from those sitting and watching. The drum went into a Thank You Song and everyone came out and shook my hand. I was smiling and I felt

Chris, wearing his regalia as he addresses the people

good, but I also kept telling myself, *You sensed her presence. It was real. Just let it be real.*

After the handshaking, the powwow went back to the business of having fun and social dancing. That's what I love about powwows. There can be a very serious moment, then we go right on with the day. Just as life should be; honor the sacred when it happens, and then enjoy and live in the ordinary.

Chris and I went back to our chairs. Chris was smoking his ever-present cigarette. I was repeating my new Lakota name

Chris and me, enjoying the Birch Coulee Gathering of Kinship

in my head—Chokta Najinn Wiŋyaŋ, Stands in the Center Woman. It made me think of being the center of attention. Just then Chris turned to me and said, "You were given a really good name."

I braved up and said, "Chris, I am feeling embarrassed about the name."

He looked shocked and asked me, "Why?"

"Well, I don't really want to be the center of attention." He looked out into the arena. The skull and other items had not been picked up yet. That was okay, as everyone knew to dance around them. There was plenty of room.

He pointed with his lips and said, "See that out there. The skull, the pipe, and other sacred items? That is the Center; it's like an altar. Lakotas call it the Center. That is your place, next to that Center, Stands in the Center Woman."

He was relaxed, enjoying his coffee and cigarette, and I could only mutter, "Thank you, Chris."

He said, "It's not me. The woman from the Eagle Nation named you." I breathed a silent prayer of thanks to her and asked for help to be worthy of that name.

The afternoon passed quickly as I returned to visiting with my new friend. It seemed so sudden when Chris said, "Time to get ready." The song had been sung for the first time just two months before. Now we were about to do something that had never been done before.

We were at Birch Coulee to bring the song out and, as Chris had said, to offer a Wiping of Tears. I put on my red velvet traditional cloth dress, my third outfit. I felt good that I made it, good that I was dressed appropriately. But as I waited to be told what to do, familiar self-doubt and anxiety began to creep into my mind and body. Many of the people at this pow-wow were elders, and many spoke Lakota. I started thinking about how they might see me: an Indian who didn't know her language, who had been around her own relatives for only twelve years. I knew some of them would be thinking, *Look at her, raised white and now comes back, got an elder to listen to her, and now thinks she is all wakan (sacred). It figures that someone who doesn't know anything will try to act like she's something and knows more than we do.*

My throat dried up and my heart was racing. I felt like bolting. I tried not to reveal all the fear that was inside me. I prayed, "Creator, help me. Am I in the right place? What do I do?"

And my answer was revealed. I saw the veterans standing on the other side of the announcer's stand. I had come in the grand entry with them and shook their hands. There is a special camaraderie among veterans that gave me an idea. I went over to the commander of the Gordon Weston Lodge Color Guard and gave him tobacco, and asked him if they could help me. We needed help in carrying items for the ceremony to the center and putting everything away when we were done. But I also asked them if they would stand outside the circle during the ceremony, as a witness to the adoptees coming home, dance in place, and shake the adoptees' hands the next time they see them. They said, "Yes. We'd be happy to help."

In my heart I was gripped with fear. But I also kept thinking that there had to be adoptees, and certainly birth parents and other relatives of adoptees and fostered individuals, at the powwow. Out of my desire for them to hear this song and begin to have that sense of belonging and relief, I walked through my fear and took my place in the center, where we had placed a large buffalo skull facing east, along with other sacred objects, on a blanket. I relaxed some as I looked over at the color guard. Four of them assumed their positions at each of the four directions, and the others were around the outside of the circle. I saw them stand at attention in all their strength and pride. They gave me the courage to go on.

Chris, Jerry, and I began the way we did at the Black Hills. Chris talked about the Indian Child Welfare Act, being on the board of the National Indian Child Welfare Association, and how the time has come to welcome home those who are making their way back, time to heal the extended family.

Then it was my turn. I breathed a quick "Help me, Creator" and reminded myself that there were adoptees there, there were birth relatives there. I told my story—the three-minute version—and I talked about how it was the drum, songs, and ceremonies that brought me home to myself and healed me. I shared that I wanted adoptees and fostered people to have a sense of belonging. That I hoped that our mothers, fathers, grandparents, and all our other relatives would heal from being separated from family, culture, and community.

Then Jerry took his turn and talked about Chris asking him to make a song. Once again, he told how he procrastinated the making of the song until it came to him. Then he explained what we were going to do, how we wanted adoptees and those who had been in foster care, and birth mothers, fathers, grandparents, brothers, sisters, aunts, uncles, cousins, to come into the center. He said, "We are going to offer you water, wipe you down, and pray with you with the pipe. Come on out to the center; this song is for you."

Chris had me stand near the blanket, where I would offer water to those who came into the circle and then show them where to stand. He stood nearby, holding his eagle wing and looking relaxed, but clearly praying. He wore a blue calico ribbon shirt, a beaded medallion, jeans, and moccasins. He had his white hair pulled back into a ponytail. Jerry sang the song through one time, then sat with the drum as they sang the Wablenica Song.

We waited for what seemed like forever. No one was coming out, and I began to say to myself, *Well, maybe I am wrong. Maybe there are no adoptees or birth mothers or fathers or other relatives here.* Then a young woman walked into the circle with her head down. She came up to me and began to cry. I hugged her and said, "You are not alone. Welcome home." After that, others began to slowly walk into the arena and formed a line as I hugged and welcomed each one home.

Then standing in front of me was the jingle dress dancer I had been talking and laughing with all afternoon. She told me through deep sobs about a brother that she and her family had been trying to find for years. "You know, we lost our brother, and we still can't find him. We keep looking for him . . ." and her words trailed off as she cried.

I said, "We will pray for him tonight."

She nodded her head and said, "Thank you."

We had just been laughing and enjoying the powwow. I would never have known her secret pain—the pain that someone has to carry inside, the pain of a lost relative. When you don't have any relief, any place to put it, it festers.

It was just incredible. The grandmas that came out, the elders that came out—it all touched me so deeply. After everyone was wiped down, given a sip of water, and then able to smoke the pipe, the song picked up to the round dance, and we all danced to the end of the song. Now laughter and happiness filled the air, replacing the hurt and pain that was just revealed. All of those who came out opened their pain to the medicine in the sage, water, and pipe. The song served to fill that part of our hearts where no words can go. The very land where their ancestors' blood had been shed is now where the individual, family, and community find healing.

When it was over, we went back to the hotel, and I fell asleep as soon as I lay down. It was so emotional that it physically drained me, yet my spirit was still dancing to the Wablenica Song.

The next day the people were abuzz. People who weren't there the night before had heard about the ceremony. "When are you going to do this again? We have never seen anything like this. How did you come up with it?"

One man said to me, "Have you heard of Gene Thin Elk? You should present something like this at his Red Road Gathering." I had heard of Gene Thin Elk, but there was no way I was going to call him to suggest that I come and talk at his gathering! Who am I?

Chris and I explained that it came from a vision. I laughed because I didn't know what I was doing. I explained that I was just following Chris—he knows what he's doing. But then Chris said, "I am just helping you with your vision." Many asked us when we were going to do it again. I hadn't thought about that. Chris said, "Well, we'll probably do it again in Mankato, because there's a powwow there in a couple of weeks." And we did.

It was the beginning of the beginning.

9

Defining a Movement

THINGS BEGAN HAPPENING, QUICKLY, as if they were meant to.

In the fall of 2000, Chris suggested that I make a presentation to the NICWA board. While some of its members no doubt heard what we said at their powwow in Tucson that spring, this would be a formal presentation. The board was meeting during a National Congress of American Indians (NCAI) conference in St. Paul, Minnesota. NCAI was formed in 1944 with one hundred people from tribes across the United States coming together in response to termination and assimilation policies that broke treaties. They worked to secure sovereign rights for today's people and their descendants. Today, NCAI is headquartered in Washington, DC, where it monitors federal policy.

I walked into the board meeting somewhat intimidated, of course, but determined to get them to understand the needs of adoptees. I don't recall exactly what I said, but I did remind them, "You all wouldn't be here on this board if it were not for adoptees. We're why you exist." Some of the board members teared up; I wondered if one person who held their head down was thinking of a lost relative. My message was well received, and the board gave me a lot of encouragement to move forward.

After the meeting I saw a friend, Carol Ann Heart. Carol

was from Rosebud and on the board of the National Indian Education Association. She wanted to know what I was doing at the conference, and I told her of the vision, the song, and the ceremonies we had done at Birch Coulee and Mankato. She said, "You should come to Aberdeen and present at the Aberdeen Area Tribal Chairmen's Health Board. They need to hear what you are doing."

In December, Chris, his friend Lisa, and I made the three-hundred-mile trip from St. Paul to Aberdeen, South Dakota. We had never been to the Aberdeen Area Tribal Chairmen's Health Board meeting, so we arrived a day before we were to present to assess the situation. The group, now called the Great Plains Tribal Chairmen's Health Board, is made up of the leaders of tribes throughout the region. I walked into the large meeting room filled with about a hundred people. The sixteen tribal chairmen or their representatives sat at a long table in the front. There were about twenty tables where those who were presenting sat facing the front table. Each of the participants took their turn telling the chairmen about their program. I noticed that they gave copies of their presentation or their program to each of the chairmen. Some were asking the board to pass resolutions supporting their work.

I went back to the hotel room and told Chris what I observed. "We need to be a program," I told him. My friend Carol Ann was there, and I asked her if she had a laptop and a floppy disc (this was before the flash drive!) that we could borrow for the night. She had someone from her office bring them to our hotel room. I made some coffee and asked Chris, "Now, what are we doing?"

He laughed and said, "I don't know."

I laughed, too. "Me either, but we should *look* like we do when we talk to the board tomorrow. Let's make some goals and objectives." Chris agreed, and I typed some things that I wanted adoptees to have if there was an organization for them. The Canadian government had offered financial support to the adoptees from their "Sixties Scoop," when about twenty thousand First Nations people were taken from their families between the late 1950s and the 1980s. They had programs that helped people search for birth relatives and offered other support to adoptees. I borrowed some ideas from the Family Reunification Program in British Columbia, too.

Our first goal was to develop strategies to address post-adoption issues and to provide service to our Stolen Generation in accordance with our traditional spiritual practices and in compliance with federal policy under the Indian Child Welfare Act.

Our second goal was to communicate a healing process to our people: to consult with tribes, communities, and agencies to develop a network of support to enhance the delivery of programs in the area of pre- and post-adoption advocacy services.

Then I said, "Okay, now we need a name. Maybe Native American Adoptee Association?"

Chris said, "No, don't use Native American. Say First Nations. We are First Nations people. We need to take back our power in who we are as Indian people. Use First Nations because it says who we are. We were here first; we are First Nations people."

I agreed. "First Nations Adoptee Association."

Then he said, "No, don't use adoptee. If you are going to talk with the grassroots people, they won't know what you're talking about. Indian languages don't have words for adoptees. The closest in Lakota is wablenica—the word for orphan. So it should be the First Nations Orphan Association."

"But Chris," I began to protest. "I am not an orphan. My mother was alive when I was adopted."

"But there is no word for adopted or adopted out," he replied.

I know that Lakota words can have deeper meanings than what a non-Native speaker understands in a simple translation. "What does wablenica mean?" I asked.

"It means to be broken apart from, into nothing."

I paused and took that meaning into my spirit. It hit hard,

hard in truth. I said, "That is exactly how I felt all my life, Chris. I felt broken, like I had nothing and was nothing. Wablenica it is." I typed the name First Nations Orphan Association and centered it on the page. Now I said, "What is happening?"

He said, "What?" thinking we were done with our brainstorming session. I got up and made another pot of coffee.

"Something is happening, Chris. I could feel it in the Black Hills and at Birch Coulee and Mankato. Something is happening. I know it's supposed to be this way. I know I was prayed home as are others . . ." I trailed off, trying to find words in the air.

I began typing. "Coming Home . . ." I said aloud as I typed it. Then Chris said, "Wicoicage aki un kupi."

"What does that mean?" I asked.

"Generation after generation we are coming home. Wicoicage means 'generation after generation.' When we pray, we acknowledge the generation past, the generation present, and the generation yet to come." He lit a cigarette and settled back into his chair with his coffee in a gesture indicating he was done. Once again, I was stunned. I kept thinking about all that had happened to lead me on my journey back to Rosebud. I thought of the first trip home and seeing the Sundance flyer with the words, "Come and pray with us so that our children will be returned to us." I always acknowledged that it was prayer that brought me into the world, kept me here, and was leading me as I ventured into this new chapter of my life.

Wicoicage: at every ceremony since time began, our ancestors prayed this sacred truth for me, you, all of us. At each ceremony, they prayed for those yet to come. They prayed for wicozani—good health and happiness. This powerful truth humbled me. Before my feet ever touched this earth, my existence was acknowledged and prayed for.

So we became First Nations Orphan Association with the tag phrase Wicoicage Aki un kupi—Generation After Generation We Are Coming Home.

The next morning, I went to Carol's office and asked her

secretary if she could print my goals and objectives and asked if she had any clip art that I could use as a logo. She found a buffalo, centered it on the page, and put our name and phrase on it. I called the phone company and set up a second line in my home for First Nations Orphan Association.

We had already made plans for the first Welcome Home Powwow on the Menominee Reservation in October 2001. Our new secretary friend found a cool watercolor background for us to run behind the powwow information—and we had a powwow flyer! I had also typed my story to include with our program. Our secretary friend arranged the materials: a cover page with our name on it, the goals and objectives, a powwow flyer, and my story. She stapled together enough copies for each chairman. In a matter of twenty-four hours, we went from having a song, a bundle, and a ceremony to having an association.

When it was our time to present, I handed out the copies to the board members. Chris spoke in Lakota, then he told of his participation on the NICWA board and how we need to heal our extended families. I talked about the challenges facing adoptees, and their rights, and how even though this can be a difficult topic, we have songs and ceremonies to help us. We thanked them for their time.

Later that night, we went to a reception. We enjoyed the cake and visited. Chris's friend Lisa, who had been mingling with others who had presented, came over to us and said, "You should have them pass a resolution. Many of the others are getting their resolutions in order now to present tomorrow."

I was exhausted—physically and mentally shot. We had spent ten hours the previous night brainstorming and getting things in order. I also did not sleep well, as I was so anxious about making a sound presentation. Putting a resolution together was more than I thought I could do. But Lisa found a resolution template and said, "Here: all you have to do is fill it out for your organization and say what you want from the board."

I found a computer in a back office. *Where is my secretary friend when I need her?* I thought to myself. With Lisa talking me through it, we got it typed and turned it in for review the next day. The result: we got our first resolution.

The trip to Aberdeen was more successful, more productive and encouraging, than we had expected. In moments like this, I am humbled to see the Creator's plan, humbled that he chose me to be part of it, despite my doubt, fear, and insecurities.

In the summer of 2001, JoAnne Jones, the president of the Ho-Chunk Nation, was at Madison Area Technical College helping a relative with administrative tasks. They came into Minority Student Services to access resources, and after I helped them, JoAnne and I began visiting. We were having such a good visit that I walked her to her car, not wanting it to end. She asked me what I had been doing, and I told her that we were going to have the first Welcome Home Powwow at the Menominee Nation in October. She stopped and said, "Let's sit down."

We sat on the grass in the warm sun, and this busy tribal president gave me her complete attention. She wanted to hear the whole story. I told her about my vision, and she thought this was a good idea, a good way to help our relatives. She then invited me to come present to the Ho-Chunk clan leaders, to encourage them to come to the powwow and see if they had some good advice for me.

I couldn't believe it. Go to the clan leaders' meeting? What an extraordinary invitation for this transplanted adoptee!

The Ho-Chunk community is about forty-five miles from Madison on Highway 90, an easy drive. When I arrived, I sat in my car to collect my thoughts. I prayed that I wouldn't say anything offensive. The spacious community building, located in a lovely, quiet, wooded area, was no-frills concrete with tables, hard folding chairs, and a kitchen. The noise of unfolding chairs and setting up tables echoed off the concrete walls. And yet the spacious room felt so very cozy. The aroma from the kitchen soon filled the room, and everyone quieted down to hear the prayer for the cooks who prepared the food and the blessing of the food to nourish our bodies.

I introduced myself to the person who looked to be in charge of the gathering. I told him that JoAnne Jones invited me, and he said, "Oh, yes. She mentioned that you were coming. Relax and enjoy your meal, and we'll get started after everyone has eaten."

In the Ho-Chunk community, it is customary to have a male introduce a female speaker. I knew this, but I forgot to ask any of my friends to come and introduce me. Fortunately, Chuck Davis Sr., whom I had just met that summer, arrived with his mother, and he agreed to introduce me. He had been present at one of the ceremonies we did, and he could speak to what he witnessed and the intent of my work. He did a wonderful job and even rendered a beautiful song.

I stood before the clan leaders and explained that I was there to invite them to a powwow in Keshena. I gave them copies of our flyer and asked them what they would like to hear from me.

"What kind of powwow?" someone asked.

"A Welcome Home Powwow for adoptees," I replied.

"Where are you from?" a grandma asked.

"I'm from Rosebud. But I didn't grow up there. I was adopted out."

"Tell us your story," another grandma said.

"My whole life story?" I asked.

"Yes," she replied.

"That could take a while," I said, thinking I'd get off the hook.

"We got all night. No one is going anywhere," another grandma replied. One of the men stood up and got me a chair so I could sit in front of them. I sat down, thanking him. I took a deep breath and began.

I shared it all, how I was born on the Rosebud Reservation in 1953, how my adoptive family were missionaries, how they moved to Wisconsin, telling me it was so I could have a better life. I shared all the abuse, the emotional isolation, and how I made it home. I could feel the emotions in the room. This was in the beginning of my work, and I often forgot that I could be talking to birth mothers and fathers. I hope no one felt more shame because of what I shared. Today, I make sure to mention that our mothers and fathers lost us during a time when there were no resources for them and that there was often manipulation to get our newborns for childless, white couples.

Several asked me questions about my journey. Then one of the male elders said, "When you adoptees come back, you are rude, pushy, loud, disrespectful, and just want percap." He was talking about the payments some tribes give members from their casino income.

I took my time in responding. "I wish I had brought some of the emails I've received from adoptees who say, 'I would relinquish any money or land, if I could just know who I am. If I could just be enrolled in my tribe, accepted by my tribe.'" I shared this in a quiet voice, so as not to be disrespectful.

As a child, I learned to communicate in the white way, the way we adoptees learn: speak quickly, show what you know, interrupt when you want to make a point. But all these communication survival skills would be offensive, deeply disrespectful, and ultimately hurtful in this situation. It was better to speak slowly, to not say everything you know about the topic at hand, and by all means, to not interrupt anyone, especially an elder. I waited for a response from the elder who said those things, to make sure he said all he needed to say. Then I responded to the heart of his complaint.

"When we are raised in the white world, we learn competition. Competition at all levels. So you are right. We are socially rude when we come back. But we don't know we are being rude. We are doing what we learned. We are loud because being loud ensures someone pays attention. We learned that to avoid getting lost in any situation. In white society, we are not taught to respect elders. They hold no status; they are just old. We are not taught to greet everyone with a handshake, a smile. So all you said is true.

"But all this is not our fault. Think about the grandchildren here. They have been playing and entertaining themselves while we meet. Sometimes you have to go check on them. Sometimes they come and whisper something in your ear. We don't mind this. This is how they learn. As they grow, they will observe more and will eventually be the ones sitting in your place. And they will have learned how to carry themselves and to discuss difficult topics respectfully.

"Adoptees don't learn anything like this. When we come back, we are like children. I was eighteen months old when I left my Indian family. For more than thirty years, that is how old I was as an Indian. I needed to be taught as a child. You need to have the same kind of kindness and patience with us as you have for your grandchildren. I know this can be hard, because we are so institutionalized, but it is not impossible to wake our Indian heart."

The Ho-Chunk elders listened, and some talked of adoption in their families. While I wasn't aware that any came to the powwow, I was welcomed and encouraged.

I am grateful to the Menominee Indian Tribe for hosting the first Welcome Home of relatives who were separated by adoption or foster care. A busload of adoptees from Canada attended. Canadians had done significant work in Winnipeg, offering help in finding relatives and providing a gathering for adoptees. But the people had not experienced a welcome home through song and ceremony as were starting to do here.

Shay Bilchik, then the president and chief executive officer of the Child Welfare League of America, came at our request and read aloud his historic acknowledgment and apology for the league's leadership in what became the systematic removal through adoption of Indian children to primarily white homes, far from culture.*

---

*See Appendix 1.

Terry Cross, then executive director of the National Indian Child Welfare Association, brought board members who stood in support with a message of healing to the gathering.

Patty Loew, the journalist who gave me the Mother Child Rock, attended and produced an eight-minute video on the event.*

The Welcome Home Powwow was wonderful.

A couple of years later, I would have another experience that helped me understand the power of song in a new way. In February 2003, we were invited to speak at a Dakota Treaty Council meeting held at the Lower Sioux Indian Community near Morton, Minnesota. Chris said to meet him at Jackpot Junction Casino Hotel, the conference location. I was excited that they wanted to hear about adoptees and my ideas about how we can help one another, but then the realization hit me. There were going to be many elders present, and who was I to get up and speak before knowledgeable elders?

Once again, I felt fear and doubt. Treaties were about land. How did the subject of adoption fit in with the subject of treaties? My message seemed way off topic. Nevertheless, I was asked to speak, and since I was asked, I would honor the request.

The conference opened with a prayer and a song from a Dakota elder. He told the story of a song he heard when he was a little boy. He asked his father what the song was about. That was the first time he heard of The 38 Dakota who were hung in Minnesota. He brought out his hand drum and told the story of The 38, and then he sang the song he first heard as a young boy. It is a beautiful, sad, strong, sacred song.

In 1862, the Dakota people in Minnesota were starving. Their small reservation had given all its resources, their crops failed, and there were no animals to hunt. The Indian agent refused to release the annual rations he had in the warehouse,

*This can be seen at https://tinyurl.com/FirstWelcomeHomePowwow.

insisting that he had to wait until the gold payment—delayed by the Civil War—arrived. Desperate to feed their starving families, the men went beyond the reservation boundaries to hunt for food. Some young men killed a white family, and war broke out. The Dakota did not agree on this, and the division caused deep harm to the oyate. More than six hundred white settlers were killed, and we don't know how many Dakota died.

At the end of the fighting, a large camp of Dakota—including those who had opposed the fighting—was set up at what became known as Camp Release, near what is now Montevideo. Henry Sibley's army, fueled by the white settlers' fears and hostilities, tricked the starving Dakota with a promise of their overdue annuity payments. Instead, the soldiers disarmed and imprisoned nearly four hundred men, leaving the women, children, and elders without protection. The men were as young as fourteen and as old as in their seventies. All of them left behind their loved ones, not knowing if they would ever see them again. The prisoners were taken to Mankato in chains. As they passed through the streets of New Ulm, they were beaten by a mob of whites who had survived the attacks on the city. The men were then locked in a stockade and warehouse outside of Mankato.

Between November 7 and 13, 1862, the men's families—seventeen hundred Dakota women, children, and elders—were marched and beaten by mobs along the one hundred and forty miles to a concentration camp below Fort Snelling.

In Mankato, a military tribunal composed of five officers carried out illegal trials, some lasting less than five minutes, and sentenced three hundred and seven Dakota men to death, most of them for allegedly being present at a battle against the whites. The prisoners had no legal counsel and didn't understand English.

In Washington, DC, Episcopal bishop Henry Whipple visited President Abraham Lincoln and tried to explain the injustices of the policies against the Dakota. Three of the president's aides reviewed the trial transcripts under orders to convict only those guilty of rape. The aides came up with only two names, but Lincoln knew that would not calm the vengeful Minnesota people. He had the names of those suspected of killing whites added to the list. Lincoln wrote the names of thirty-nine Dakota men on White House stationery and approved their execution. One was reprieved.

The entire town of Mankato came to watch "savages" be hung, justified in their relief and satisfaction that they were rid of more "red devils." They did not know they were watching ordinary men who had been sentenced unjustly.

The Dakota men were marched into the town square with their faces painted in the traditional red and blue of warriors in battle. They lifted their song loudly to their Creator. They sang death songs, and a Christian hymn, as they were led up the oak gallows to stand over the traps on the scaffold. Their heads were covered with sacks. As they stood on the scaffold singing, they reached out and held each other's hands and blankets.

With the first swing of his ax, Captain William Duley failed to cut the rope. When he swung again, all thirty-eight Dakota men fell, calling out their names. When one of the ropes broke, Hdainyanka (Rattling Runner) was hanged a second time. Another man struggled for nearly twenty minutes before he suffocated.

They were buried nearby in a shallow grave in a sandbar by the Minnesota River. That evening doctors from nearby towns dug up their bodies and took them to study; one of those doctors was the founder of Mayo Clinic. Many of the skeletons were later tossed into the trash. Descendants of The 38 recovered a few of their ancestors' remains so their spirits could find rest. The skeletal remains of Mahpiya Te Najin (One Who Stands on a Cloud) stood disgracefully on display in Mayo Clinic's early years. One hundred thirty-six years after the execution, in 1998, the Mayo Clinic returned the remains of Mahpiya Te Najin to his family.

The next spring after the hangings, the families were sent to Crow Creek, where more of them died. The other convicted men were sent to a military post in Iowa, still under death sentences.

I knew this story, and I listened to it again in anger—an anger that made me even more determined to honor our ancestors. Those who survived these incredible times held on to the language, our songs, and ceremonies.

Just before I was to speak, a friend whom I had just met, Kenny Seaboy, gave me a card that said, "Believe in your dreams." It was just what I needed to nudge me forward, and it gave me enough courage that I sounded confident.

Then I realized there was something in the story of The 38 that I could use to connect those who were at this conference to those of our relatives who have not yet made it home.

When it was my turn to speak. I introduced myself clumsily in Lakota. You always introduce yourself with your Indian name, where you are from. It helps connect you to the listeners. Someone may approach you later and ask if you are related to someone they know, or they may share a story about an experience they had on your reservation. Traditional introductions help us keep our connections.

I shared the vision I had of welcoming our relatives home. That our relatives needed healing. I shared that I made a connection with The 38: that in their last minutes of life, these strong, proud Dakota men sang a Dakota song as they were led to the scaffold. A song! Together, in these last hours, they knew they were Dakota. They gained strength in the words of that death song. They drew strength in being together, supporting each other in this incredibly unjust hour.

They died without the comfort of family. Their wives, mothers, and grandmothers at Fort Snelling were not allowed to grieve their loved ones. They were not allowed a warrior's burial. But in their darkest moment, they had a song. A song that reminded them who they were, where they come from, and where they were going.

I gained a little confidence and realized on another level that I was on the right track, as elders nodded in agreement.

Some of the men even offered the vocable *hau* in agreement. Adoptees deserved a song that would help us, because a song can go to a place in your heart where no words can go. Words do not help that kind of pain in your soul, but the drumbeat can because when the men are singing on that drum, it is alive, and there is a spirit there. That spirit goes into your heart and takes you to that place in that circle and gives you your sense of belonging, your sense of pride, your dignity, your self-worth—all that is good in our human spirit.

An elder once said to me, "You adoptees are the last remnant of the Indian wars." Because he was an elder, I did not ask any questions. But I wondered, *Might that be just a bit of a jump? It is 2002, after all.* Now it was making sense.

The war of 1862 marked the end of the wars of the Dakota in Minnesota. It was the beginning of the boarding school era. And those who survived that era gave birth to us, the adoption generation. Children being removed systematically was another kind of war: a war of power differential in policy.

I know that as Indian people we get our strength through our Indian names. We know that we are stronger as we learn our traditions. Our strength is in our identity. We need our language, songs, and ceremonies. I think of the high suicide rates of adoptees and foster children, both present and past. I think about the ones who—right now as I write this—are contemplating ending their lives because it is just too hard to go on alone. I think about the ones who have already passed to the spirit world without ever hearing a song or the comforting sound of the drum. They died alone, without ever knowing. For those our relatives who never knew their Indian names or heard a song, let us put our hearts and minds together to honor what they gave us, their lives.

I've seen the fear, the confusion, the sadness, the uneasiness, the shame in other adoptees when they come to an Indian gathering for the first time. I've seen them stand outside that circle. I know what it's like to stand outside that circle and not know how to get inside, how to assume my place.

We have a place in that circle because that's who we are, but when you are raised outside of your identity, you don't know that. You assume shame. And that shame is the basis of all that destructive behavior in those statistics that represent my people.

10

Welcoming Them Home

THE WIPING OF TEARS CEREMONY is one of the seven sacred ceremonies given to the Lakota people. It is used to heal grief caused by the death of a relative or loved one, and it is usually done a year after the death.

Today it has been used to heal grief caused by boarding schools and domestic violence and for those who fought in war. We have also used it for all people who have been affected by adoption or foster care. Because adoption and foster care begin with the loss of connections, the loss of history that can ultimately lead to a loss of identity, everyone is affected by a placement outside of the family and culture. Mothers, fathers, grandparents, uncles, aunts, cousins, brothers, and sisters are all impacted. The removal of children breaks down the extended family, the community, and the nation of a people—the oyate.

Some traditional Lakota people have questioned the use of the Wiping of Tears Ceremony for anything other than to heal grief from the death of a loved one. I understand and want to respect our traditions and not add to or take away from what was given to us in a sacred manner. For that reason, we have stopped using the Wiping of Tears Ceremony for this purpose. What we do now is the Wablenica Ceremony—the Orphan Ceremony. We have been given what we need for a ceremony: a vision, a song, the Wopakta Wablenica Wakan

(Sacred Orphan Bundle), a pipe, a drum, an eagle wing, and a buffalo skull that sits on a star quilt. Each item was given to me through others who saw the need for healing families and communities who have been hurt by adoption and foster care.

I am often asked to describe the Wablenica Ceremony. This is exceptionally hard to do, because it's something that one has to experience. There are just no words to adequately describe the sacred. I will do my best, though, to describe the ceremony we offer for those returning.

If we are at a powwow, just as I did at Birch Coulee the first time we did the ceremony, I ask the color guard to stand in the four directions and in the circle around the dance area.

We ask jingle dress dancers to come into this circle and form another one. The jingle dress was given to the Ojibwe people during a time of hardship. A man whose daughter was very ill sought a vision and was told how to make this dress and how she should dance. After she healed, she started a Jingle Dress Dance Society. Today the jingle dress is used in many healing ceremonies. Women who dance jingle know the responsibility that comes with it and know they may be called upon at any time to dance for healing.

We invite all adoptees and fostered individuals, birth mothers and fathers, and any relative of someone who has been affected by adoption or foster care to come stand in a circle, inside these circles. I tell some of my story and tell about the vision for the song and ceremony and how Jerry Dearly made the song. I then explain what is lying in the center of the circle. On a star quilt sits a buffalo skull, an eagle wing, the Sacred Orphan Bundle given to me in the Black Hills, and the other sacred items that have been given for use in the ceremony.

I say to the adoptees and other relatives, "I was given this bundle to take care of; it is the Sacred Orphan Bundle; it belongs to each of you. It is here to encourage you, to help you heal. In my responsibility to take of it, I have Sundanced with it since 2002. During the four days of Sundance, I pray to each of the four directions and ask the grandfathers of each direction to help those who are trying to find their way home. I pray for our mothers, fathers, and other family relatives, as many of them miss us and wonder if there is something they can do to find us. This pipe you see here, this canupa wakan, sacred pipe, was made by Randy Benard, a veteran from Flandreau, South Dakota. The first time we did the ceremony, I had a lot of fear about how the people would react to it. I asked the Gordon Weston Lodge Color Guard to help me by standing in this ceremony. Randy is a member, and he made this pipe and gave it to me to use when we do this ceremony. It is a black stone from Canada. I take care of this pipe and pray with it every year at Sundance. This pipe is for you, for your healing.

"Every year since June 21, 2000, I have prayed for adoptees. But before I prayed, your communities have prayed for you. Every time there is a ceremony, as Indian people we acknowledge those who came before us, those who are here now, and those yet to come. So, my friends, you were prayed for before you ever placed your feet on Mother Earth. You were never forgotten, and while it may have felt lonely out there, you were never alone. Now all that we are going to do is for you, this song, this pipe, this bundle, this ceremony is for you, for your healing."

By now the cloud of sadness begins to rise and hover above everyone in the circle and lingers from their shoulders up, as most stand with their heads hung down.

We share the pipe around the circle, so everyone in the circle can smoke it. The smoke carries the prayers from our hearts. We remind everyone that we do not need to be ashamed. There is so much behind the loss of our children. So many mothers were not encouraged or helped during the time they needed it the most. Some made the decision to give their child away only to deeply regret it later. Many fathers were totally left out of the decision-making. Children feel they were given away because there was something wrong with them. Many have spent years in isolation and confusion before they make it home to put the pieces back together. We use the drum, songs, and ceremony to heal the heart, mind, and body.

Heads are still hung low; those who do look forward have a mixture of pain and sadness on their faces. As the pipe is shared, a drum group sings the Wablenica Song and the jingle dress dancers weave in and out of the circle, using their eagle feather fans to "wipe off" the smog of shame, sadness, and hurt from the shoulders of all who stand in the circle. Most people go through life never putting words to this kind of pain. In the Wablenica Ceremony, we can stand in the circle, open that part of our heart, and let the medicine of smoke from the sage, the sound of the drum, and the song go into that dark place and begin healing.

Once everyone has smoked the pipe, we share closing words. Community members who have witnessed the ceremony come out and shake hands and hug those in the ceremony. And then those in the ceremony and the community form a large circle, and we round dance together. By now, faces are lit up with smiles and laughter as we dance together.

The community plays an important part in the ceremony, as they stand in witness of those who are coming home to the Indian community and home to themselves. Their welcome home handshake and encouragement is the nurturing many have been looking for for so long. Everyone walks away with a sense of well-being, having brought their sadness, shame, and guilt to the circle and leaving it there to walk in the balance of pride and dignity with a sense of belonging, as our ancestors have prayed for us.

PART 3

Reconciliation

11

Reconciliation Begins
with the Individual

WHEN I BEGAN TALKING ABOUT Truth and Reconciliation, I heard people in our communities say, "What do we have to reconcile? We didn't do anything; it was done *to* us." And, "In order to be reconciled, we have to have been 'conciled.' Our communities have never been in any kind of agreement." And, "We can never be reconciled to genocide."

What communities want is justice and restoration. That makes sense. I always thought that is what reconciliation is: justice and restoration. When you gather statements to compile findings, the findings lead to recommendations of how to address the statements. So, if we call it Truth, Healing, Reconciliation or Truth, Healing, and Justice, it is still bringing together two seemingly incompatible groups (those who have been harmed and those who caused the harm) with the goal of reaching agreement on addressing legal, moral, and ethical wrongs, violations of human rights, and assaults on dignity. Righting wrongs requires both acknowledgment and action. If the terms Truth and Justice speak more clearly to the people in a community, then that is what should be used in that community.

Words matter. My cousin LeMoine LaPointe shared, "We must choose our words carefully. We can either give life or take life with our words." In the spirit of that teaching, may my words give life to this process.

I was having breakfast with Eileen Hudon, an Ojibwe elder from the White Earth Nation. She started telling me about her work as a sexual abuse survivors' activist, and it was so interesting that I ate my whole meal while she talked. Then I told her, "Eileen, you can eat now, and I'll talk." We laughed, then waved the waitress down so she could reheat Eileen's breakfast.

I began to talk about how hard it is for adoptees to forgive, that forgiveness is a difficult concept to understand when you have been violated as a child. I shared my story about how I was angry for so long and how I was told I had to forgive my adoptive mother. I gritted my teeth whenever I heard those words: "You *have* to forgive." The very thought of doing that brought raw pain to my spirit.

Eileen couldn't wait till she was done eating. "I was at a conference where the spiritual leader was talking about forgiveness and said that in order to heal you have to forgive. Finally, I raised my hand and asked, 'What is the Ojibwe word for forgiveness?' He sat back in his chair, folded his arms over his belly, and stared down at the floor, thinking. Then his folded arms started bouncing up and down as he chuckled and through a smile said, 'There is no word for forgiveness. The closest we have is compassion.'"

I had to interrupt and tell her my story. When I was first meeting Indian people, I was having a discussion with a Lakota elder, a grandmother. I told her my story of being taken away, how I was abused, and how I was lied to about not being wanted. I recall that I had a lot of anger in my voice.

She listened, then told me, "As Lakota people we live with certain values. One of them is wounsila [wah-OON-shee-la], compassion. If we are Lakota, even those who hurt us, we have compassion for them." I was stunned. Compassion?

How and why would I have compassion for the woman who lied to me and hurt me? I was quiet after she said that. That thought joined the others in that drawer with all the things I didn't know what to do with. Eileen and I looked at each other and saw that we were indeed relatives.

Years later, after I prayed in the sweat lodge and listened to our teachings, compassion began to enter my heart. It entered after I began to extend compassion to myself. Compassion to understand that I was abusive until I learned to be a loving mother, and compassion to heal other hurts in my spirit. I started seeing my adoptive mother as someone who was broken, scared, and pitiful. She couldn't give me what she didn't have. To continue to be angry with her about that would be fruitless. She just did not have that to give.

I can't tell you when it happened, how it happened. It just happened. Compassion slipped into the back door of my heart when it knew that I would not kick it out. It was as if it knew that I would want it to stay—and I would also invite in its relatives: healing and generosity.

Reconciliation is a process, not an event. It begins within an individual. Mine began the first time I went home to Rosebud. I had to reconcile the story I was told growing up with the story my family members told me. That process was difficult. It led me to question the Creator, and even made me wonder why I was working so hard to remain sober. Why work hard at living an emotionally honest life when my life had been a lie in stories and a lie on paper?

I wasn't aware that it was reconciliation. I was just doing the work to put my two seemingly opposing realities together, to bring balance. So much anger to work through, so much pain to feel. Sorting and sorting, feeling and letting go, taking it back, trying not to be resentful, letting go. Trying not to feel sorry for myself, letting go. Trying to understand how anger was making me become the ugliness I endured growing up, letting go. Then, finally to letting go and setting it down, no need to pick it up again.

The reconciliation process will serve to guide you to a solution you are seeking. Fair warning—it most likely will not look like what you expected.

What is reconciliation? What does reconciliation mean? In English, reconciliation means to restore to friendship; to settle or resolve differences; to make consistent or congruous; to cause to submit to, or accept, something unpleasant; to account for.

When we look at what it takes to restore and address wrongs, the Indian community plays a vital role in reconciliation. When community members open the wounds and talk about the damage caused by child removal through boarding school, adoption, and foster care, those who represent the government and other institutions can see and hear about the long-term impacts for themselves. When we can hold that truth in a circle of compassion, healing can begin. When the healing begins, reconciliation starts. When these two seemingly incompatible things come together, the work of finding balance can begin.

Reconciliation begins with the individual. It is the individual interacting with others, respectfully listening to see how they can be part of a solution to move forward.

12

The Work

OUR WORK TOOK MANY FORMS, but they were all connected by talking, listening, and using ceremony to heal ourselves and others. Tina Knafla, a social worker in the adoptions unit of Hennepin County, saw a healing ceremony we did at the 2002 NICWA conference, and she wanted to have one in Minneapolis. Several individuals from the various Indian organizations joined the planning committee, and the Minneapolis American Indian Center sponsored the powwow. Jacque Wilson, Bois Forte Ojibwe, was working at the Indian Center at that time. The powwow was named through a group decision: The Gathering for Our Children and Returning Adoptees Powwow. The planners wanted to celebrate children and welcome relatives back to the circle. I was still living in Wisconsin, so I attended only a few of the planning meetings.

The first powwow was a success and the community response was positive. A young Indian girl was present with her foster parents. She had some major health issues, and the family was on their way to Mayo Clinic. At Chris's direction, we did a healing for her with the jingle dress dancers. It was a beautiful moment of nurturing this young girl with our song and ceremony.

After I moved to Minnesota, I assumed the role of pulling planners together each year for the powwow. Tina and

With Chris and Jerry at The Gathering for Our Children and Returning Adoptees Powwow

Jacque stayed on to plan and work the powwow each year. Adoptees travel from all over the country to meet other adoptees and find that sense of belonging. Members of the Minneapolis Indian community provide healing at the end of the ceremony by shaking hands or hugging—and by saying, "Welcome home." Those two words are so very powerful. There are no words to describe it. The overpowering experience of isolation is lifted by a community member, a relative, saying, "Welcome home."

I had become somewhat more comfortable leading the ceremony over time. I knew how to set up the center, make sure everything was in place. It was getting easier to quiet the doubts that fueled my anxieties. When we did the ceremony again at Birch Coulee in September 2003, I had started to understand this is what I was supposed to be doing, and I was grateful to be part of this healing time.

The community responded, and as the ceremony ended with the warm handshakes, hugs, and laughter, I walked back to my chair. On the way, a woman stopped me, shook my hand, and said, "I really liked what I just saw. Social workers like me need to hear this." Without asking, I knew what she meant. They needed to hear about the great wound in our community left by the systematic removal of our children. "Do you do trainings?" she asked.

Without blinking I said, "Yes, I do trainings." I lied. Well, not completely: I had done diversity trainings when I was working at Madison Area Technical College. I knew she meant social work trainings, but I thought to myself, *I can do that.*

The seed began to sprout. A month later, I talked with Jerry and Chris about the discussion with the social worker. I told them I wanted to hold a forum, to bring adoptees, fostered individuals, and other birth relatives together with all those who played a role in deciding to remove a child from an Indian family: social workers, guardians ad litem (people appointed to represent the children in court), lawyers, judges. I wanted the people who had been affected by adoption and foster care to tell the professionals about their lived experiences. I wanted the professionals to hear what it was like to grow up away from our culture, separated from our families. I specifically did not want the professionals to counsel us or feel like they had to fix those telling the stories. I hoped they would learn from our experiences and think about us as they worked with families.

Jerry and Chris thought this was a good idea, and they said they would help me with it. Right after this conversation, we traveled to Crow Creek Reservation in South Dakota. We were invited to speak to a group of about twenty elders, mostly grandmothers, who gathered in a meeting room at the Lodestar Casino Hotel. White-haired and round, they sat with their hands resting on their stomachs, their soft brown fingers intertwined, ready to listen. I told them my story. I saw the grandmothers' shoulders tense with anxiety. They listened intently as I told the story of my vision for a song and how it was sung for the first time. Still, this sadness in their faces hurt my heart.

I realized there were probably birth mothers in this group. After a pause, I said, "On behalf of adoptees who may have come from your reservation, I say, thank you for giving us the most sacred gift of all. Thank you for giving us life. Please forgive yourselves and know we are happy that we have life and that we are here." I saw shoulders relax and brows un-crinkle; some even nodded their heads, ever so slightly.

I continued to share that we can heal this hurt in our people; that I hoped when their relatives make it back to their community, they would welcome them home.

To change the subject and show how we can use our stories to educate, I talked about meeting the social worker at Birch Coulee and our plans to bring adoptees and fostered individuals together to tell their stories. I told them we were about to have our first Truth and Reconciliation Community Forum.

A voice spoke up in the group. "Don't say 'Truth and Reconciliation' without including 'Healing.' If you don't make time for healing, there will be no reconciliation. There was a year of reconciliation here in South Dakota in 1990. No one came to hear our stories—there was no healing—there was no reconciliation."*

It made so much sense to me. But how was I going to do this?

*   *   *

----

*A hundred years after the massacre at Wounded Knee, South Dakota governor George Mickelson and representatives of South Dakota's nine tribal governments proclaimed 1990 a Year of Reconciliation and called for the first Native American Day observance to honor Native Americans. It was held on December 29, 1990, the anniversary of the massacre.

In 2004, George McCauley and I were married and living in Minneapolis. He worked at the Minneapolis American Indian Center, and one day he told me, "I think your relative is working at the Indian Center."

We had met LeMoine LaPointe at a funeral in South Dakota the previous year. George reintroduced himself, and we had dinner with LeMoine and his family. LeMoine told me that he knew about me. He said he and my brother Leonard called each other *brother,* even though in the white way they were cousins. He also welcomed me home. Even though I had been home for fourteen years by then, it felt wonderfully healing to have another relative say, "Welcome home. We are your family. I am glad to finally see you."

A couple of weeks after this dinner, feeling as apprehensive as ever, I passed tobacco to LeMoine and asked him to help me with the forum. He was now the director of the Healthy Nations Program at the Minneapolis American Indian Center, but he had been working for decades to bring experiential learning to Lakota children who were being lost in the system. LeMoine accepted the tobacco and agreed to come and help. I told him my goal for the forum was for adoptees to have the opportunity to tell a part of their story that they would want social workers to hear. I wanted social workers to hear, from the people themselves, about the long-term effects on individuals who had been separated from their families and cultures.

We held the first forum in February 2006 at the Minnesota Indian Women's Resource Center in Minneapolis. I advertised it on the University of Minnesota's Minnesota Indian listserv and in *The Circle,* a local Indian newspaper. I didn't want cost to be a deterrent for any adoptees wanting to attend, so I asked those who could to donate $25 to cover expenses; we presenters donated our time. Registrations began to come in from Duluth, South Dakota, Wisconsin, and Illinois, including someone who wanted to meet adoptees to interview for her research. There were about fifty in all, including quite a few social work professionals, which surprised me. I wanted them to be there, but I still had doubts that the professional community really cared what happened after their decisions were made. When you have suffered as a result of someone's decision, it is very easy to see everyone like them as agents of harm.

I bought seventy-two pieces of cooked chicken from Cub Foods and cooked a huge roaster full of goulash. My stepdaughter contributed her famous chocolate-covered Rice Krispies treats. My cousin Martha ordered a beautiful cake with "Generation After Generation We Are Coming Home" on it. I brought my own thirty-cup coffee maker, Styrofoam cups, and some pop and water. After the purchase of paper products and other necessities, the cost was around $250.

On that Saturday morning, I loaded up my van and drove to the center. I was excited and nervous all at once.

The facility has a small basement gym with high windows above our reach. There are huge mural paintings of jingle dress dancers on the main wall. It has a small kitchen with a serving window.

Those who arrived early helped me carry in the food and set up. We arranged the chairs in a large circle with an opening facing the murals. We placed a small table there, with our sacred items to be used in the ceremony, our notes, and a borrowed microphone and speaker. It was truly a humble, grassroots beginning.

As Chris surveyed the setup, he said, "Put the Orphan Bundle in the center along with the Eagle Staff. It will help us throughout the day."

When it was finally time to start, Jerry called everyone together in his commanding yet respectful voice, and the first community forum—the first Truth Healing Reconciliation Forum—began. He sang a song and got everyone to laugh. As a teacher of the Lakota language, he naturally gave everyone a language lesson in Lakota greetings. When everyone seemed relaxed, he introduced Chris as our respected elder.

Chris began to speak in his quiet voice, delivering powerful words. I heard again that phrase that will stay with me forever, as we need to be reminded, "Pray along with me in your own language, pray from your heart not your head. Your head will always get you in trouble, but your heart is where all wisdom lays." He then asked the spirits to bless our day.

Jerry took the microphone and explained what was going to happen in the order of the day. He is a gifted announcer, and he knows how to transition a group. He introduced LeMoine and said, "I am not sure what LeMoine is going to do, but I am sure *he* knows, and I am sure we will enjoy it." He was telling the truth. None of us had any idea what was coming next. As I put the schedule together, I had not talked to LeMoine, Jerry, or Chris about what they would contribute. I trusted that they could fill in with their skills. After all, it was the first one. We could only plan so much.

LeMoine stood at the circle opening and introduced himself. "My name is LeMoine LaPointe. I am from a small community in Rosebud called Little Crow's Camp. I am Sandy's cousin. We just met a few weeks ago. I grew up with her brother. We called ourselves brothers, even though in the white way we are cousins, but we didn't know any different. We were brothers. It took me fifty years to be reunited with my relative. It makes me happy to know her, and I am happy she is home."

He said his contribution would be to get everyone acquainted, and he asked everyone to count off in twos. Before we knew it, he had everyone in two circles, an outer circle and an inner circle, with the participants facing each other. He asked everyone to introduce themselves and share one thing that happened to them that was really funny. It could be anything, from any time in their lives. "Everyone in the inner circle, stay put, and everyone on the outside, after you have introduced yourselves, the ones in the outer circle move clockwise to the next person. We will do this until everyone has shaken hands and introduced themselves."

Soon the room was full of loud chatter, some people bent over with laughter and others with eyes popping and hands clasped over their mouths as if to say, "No way." This exercise set the tone of the day. It disarmed anxiety and laid the foundation for relationships. LeMoine's guidance was so respectful and gentle. His skill was obvious.

Jerry, Chris, and I were watching all this from the side. Jerry looked at me and said, "Wow, he's good."

I answered, "I had no idea he could do this. I just knew I was supposed to ask him to work with us."

Chris said, "He is one of us now."

At the end of the day, as I was loading my van, LeMoine thanked me for asking him to help and said it was one of the most rewarding things he had done.

The forum was a success beyond my expectations. There were about sixty participants: adoptees, fostered individuals, social workers, lawyers, mental health workers, guardians ad litem, a director of an adoption project, and Hennepin County's director of Indian Child Welfare. We went around the circle, first asking the adoptees, "What is one thing you want social workers to know about your adoption?" We asked the social workers to listen. Late in the afternoon, we had the social workers, guardians ad litem, adoption workers, and other professionals share one thing they learned. One guardian ad litem said, "This will forever change how I advocate for Indian children." At the end of the forum, Daniel Nelson Fox, one of the adoptees, told me that some of the adoptees wanted to get together on a regular basis to talk. Nelson also emailed me to give encouragement for the event. He talked about how much healing had happened that day.

Not long after the first forum, I was asked to provide a forum for Hennepin County's Indian Child Welfare program and their foster families and adoptive families.

I have watched forum participants, both those impacted by the child welfare system and those who make the decisions about families. It is an honor to watch the professionals courageously recount systematic judgments that were not centered in family preservation but rather focused on family destruction. I say "destruction" because it reflects the way harm to one family brings subsequent harm to the next generation. That is a destruction. That is a disruption during a family's time of deepest need, whether it be struggling with the disease of addiction, with being unsheltered, or with not being able to find gainful employment. All of these are issues that can be addressed with concentrated resources.

At first, I didn't want white people to express their feelings of grief when they understand what has happened in the name of social work—or to talk about their feelings of guilt and shame for how they had viewed the families they were working with. They also didn't get to do therapy or counsel other participants. But then I realized that if we are going to invite people to our circles, we have a responsibility to take care of all invited. That balance of care means the white guilt or shame will not overshadow the generational grief that is expressed. Those who make the decisions are participants witnessing the outcome of their decisions—decisions that were supposed to bring the children safety and permanency, and instead brought the family years of abuse.

After the first forum, every month or so, Nelson sent me an email with a gentle nudge to remind me of the need for local adoptees to get together and encourage one another. I was beginning to travel a lot, and Nelson would always say, "I know you're busy. I pray for you all the time and look forward to when we can meet as a group."

I knew he was right. I listened once to a mother's story. Through her tears, she choked out these words, recounting a dream she had of her child who had been removed on an "administrative technicality"—the court's word. With eyes cast down in shame that didn't belong to her, she said, "I wanted to see her. I was looking for her. I guess I was searching for her in my dreams."

After listening to her grief, I found myself at a loss for words that could offer any solace. But this kind of pain needs to be expressed, witnessed, and acknowledged before it can subside. This is true for others, as well, and it's complicated. When adoptees return to their birth mothers, fathers, or communities, they are the mirror of the original trauma of their removal. Those who they first meet can be really excited, but then the painful feelings that were buried can resurface and become unbearable, and the swirl of emotions creates distance once again.

Adoptees can face personal dilemmas in their established relationships. One adoptee had found her Native family and siblings, and this reunion had begun to fill the void she felt, wondering where she came from and who she is. Sadly, she admitted, "My husband asked me, 'When are you going to get over this?'"

Many adoptees' partners do not understand that they really married a person of color, not a white person. Once the adoptee begins to understand that and actually become who they are, the partners find themselves in an interracial marriage. For some, this is a major shock. If they are unable to resolve this huge development in identity, their marriages sometimes end.

After a few months of Nelson's emails, I finally contacted Marlene Helgamo, the pastor of All Nations Church in Minneapolis. She lets the community use the sanctuary for meetings. It is a perfect setup: off to the side of the sanctuary is a full kitchen with a large serving window.

Marlene was kind enough to allow us to use the church in exchange for a small donation of supplies. We have met on the first Thursday of the month since 2006 for a potluck and talking circle. Our group has been attended by as many as fifteen to as few as two. But no matter the size, a miraculous thing occurs. Someone realizes they are not alone, that others have prayed for them, and most of all, that their story matters—and healing takes place.

There is also unexpected humor. As one adoptee was telling his story and describing how he began understanding who he is as an Indian person, he paused and said, "Do you want to know how white I was?" The group of adoptees listening laughed hard, heads falling back in open-mouthed roars of laughter—seeing themselves.

Humor expressed in the circle neutralizes shame by exposing it to the love of others who have done the same thing. Being able to laugh at ourselves in a good way is truly Indian humor. That laughter keeps the spirit alive and our circles strong. We laughed, teasing each other about how we were all afraid.

Because there was no organized effort at a local, state, national, or international level to address the needs of people separated from their cultures by foster care or adoption, our work grew. I began to travel, invited and funded by organizations and tribes in other regions who had heard about the ceremony and the forums. In some years, I did three or four presentations each month.

But I also wanted to focus on research as well as advocacy and education. In 2012, I thought it was time to change the name from First Nations Orphan Association to First Nations Repatriation Institute and incorporate as a nonprofit.

FNRI collaborates with people in the indigenous community, service providers, advocates, educators, researchers, policy makers, and others. It is a resource for First Nations people impacted by foster care or adoption who seek to return home, reconnect, and reclaim their identity. The institute also works to enhance the knowledge and skills of practitioners who serve First Nations people. It works with a research team at the University of Minnesota to provide the research, data, and vetted studies that are needed to argue for more resources and better policies relating to adoptees and fostered individuals.

The institute's goal is to promote Truth, Healing, and Reconciliation through providing education for social workers and others in the community; participating and hosting regional and national conferences; and bringing together legal professionals, social workers, educators, and other professionals through hosting a National Repatriation Forum. To attract Native scholars, we offer internships to students who work with the University of Minnesota research team on FNRI research projects. They gain undergraduate and graduate credit while accomplishing work relevant to First Nations people.

While this work keeps us busy, there is more to be done. Funding to support presentations at local, state, national, and international conferences; funding to develop a research agenda and support graduate research; publications in peer-reviewed journals; collaborations with other organizations to influence public policy; a clearinghouse and repository of psychosocial, spiritual, and legal resources—the possibilities are clear and exciting.

13

Words of Witness

IN CEREMONY, IN FORUMS, and in talking circles, adoptees find what they need. In this chapter, they speak for themselves.

We began the work in the song and ceremony that became the Wablenica Ceremony, the Orphan Ceremony, usually held at a powwow.

● "The powwow and ceremony helped to heal my wounds, gave me hope for the future, and brought me closer to my son."
Patrick Day, Lac du Flambeau adoptee

● "The ceremony brought me back into a world that was taken away from me at birth. It gave me my identity back. Even if I never meet them, it brought my family back."
Jan Rootes, White Earth Ojibwe adoptee

● "It never mattered to me that I'd already returned home to my family on the Peigan reserve in Alberta twenty years before having met Sandy. What she brought to us adoptees was a gift from our community of respect and honor. Though I knew many people at the powwow after having lived and provided services in the community, it was yet another moment of great vulnerability for me. You see, I'd come to feel accepted as an Indian person just by being. Years ago, when I first returned home, I struggled so greatly, feeling I had to prove myself in some manner, even to my own people, to gain their acceptance and have them claim me.

"What would they think of me now, knowing I'd grown up outside of my community in the white world? As the community stood in line to shake my hand and those of the other adoptees and I listened to those sacred jingle dresses just beyond the line of people welcoming me, those feelings of insecurity seemed so insignificant in the shadow of such respect and honoring I, we, felt that day at the Gathering for Our Children and Returning Adoptees Powwow. There are those who simply do not have the personal strength to leave the safety of the crowd in the stands to be welcomed, but as they continue to see us, maybe, just maybe, they'll be standing with us next year or the year after. Even if they never do, they'll always know, they are not alone."

Kirk Crowshoe, Blackfoot adoptee, American Indian liaison at the Minnesota Department of Employment and Economic Development

● "I participated in the ceremony about the year 2000 at a Mahkato powwow. It felt good to be a part of the ceremony. It seemed like for a while I was walking off balance a little bit, during that time in my life. I was still trying to fill a void and find acceptance within myself and my heart with regard to my past, my anger, and everything that I struggled with internally. I felt like I didn't know where my place was in the circle, and I felt lost.

"That ceremony started to help me by making me realize that what happened to me being fostered/adopted out was MY road that I had to take. That this experience was for me, and I was to learn from it and come back to the circle and to my Dakota tiwahe and oyate to help other people. I learned how to pray, I am learning my language, and I have done some healing. I now understand that it is time for me to give back. I thank Creator for those experiences, and for each day of life and the lessons that have been given and are yet to come."

Naida Medicine Crow, Dakota adoptee

● "The annual event has something to offer everyone who attends, because the focus is on healing, it touches all, not only adoptees but families who lost relatives. The ceremony itself has the power to provide closure and beginning in the same moment."

   Lisa (LaCroix) Weddell, Wachante Ognaka Win, Dakota Oyate adoptee

● "I've been to powwows before, but this one was different. The entrance read, 'Gathering for Our Children and Returning Adoptees.' The annual powwow was in its ninth year at the Minneapolis American Indian Center, and it is a collaboration between the Department of Human Services, Hennepin County ICWA Unit's Tina Knafla, and Jacque Wilson, as well as my aunt Sandy White Hawk, director of the First Nations Repatriation Institute. The goal is to reconnect adoptees with their families and culture as well as raise awareness of the need for Native foster/adoptive homes. My heart smiled at seeing my auntie and cousins. For the last several years, I'd been on a quest to find the rest of my Lakota family.

   "My family history follows a common theme in Indian country: assimilation. My mom was one of nine children born to my Sicangu Lakota grandmother, Nina Lulu White Hawk, on the Rosebud Sioux Reservation. Before the protections of the Indian Child Welfare Act (ICWA), social workers broke into my grandmother's house when she wasn't home, stole her children, and flung them to the winds.

   "My mom and three of her siblings were placed in an orphanage in Nebraska.

   "Into my generation, none of us were allowed to be Native growing up . . . but over the years we were able to connect with many of our relatives, thanks to my mom's sister, my aunt Deb.

   "At the adoptee powwow, I hopped down the bleachers filled with a couple hundred onlookers to join the circle of returning adoptees preparing for the healing ceremony. Suddenly I felt a knot growing in my throat. *Crap*, I thought. *I'm going to cry before the ceremony even starts.*

"Sage smoke filled the air. I stood with the other adoptees in a circle, surrounded by a ring of jingle dress dancers followed by a ring of veterans. I gazed across the group to see a visibly distraught woman tightly clutching her shawl and choking back sobs. Her eyes were swollen and red from crying.

"The drum group started to sing a healing song. The jingle dress dancers began their sacred footwork, waving their eagle feather fans over us. They swayed and dipped. Tingles shot down my spine with every fan that touched my shoulders. Then I lost it. Tears flowed uncontrollably. Every tear represented a moment I felt lost, afraid, angry, frustrated, empty, and confused. . . . But I was comforted by the swish of the jingles mimicking the sound of water, the sound of healing. And slowly my emotional burden started to fade. As the tears fell to the ground, I felt lighter. When the singing stopped, I felt a sense of renewal. Crying is medicine.

"After the ceremony, we gathered upstairs for an adoptee talking circle. We each reflected on our experience. Several adoptees commented that the powwow was unlike any other they'd been to. Even though so many of our Native children were lost through adoption, many tribes don't yet have a powwow or ceremony to acknowledge their return. But the adoptees felt welcome at Aunt Sandy's powwow; they felt like they were finally coming home to a community. One older man commented he felt the gaping, empty hole inside him start to fill up to form a complete person.

"I hope more adoptees and relatives of adoptees will find a way to join us at the powwow—especially for the end of the ceremony, when community members stream down to shake our hands and say with a warm embrace, 'Welcome home.'"

Racheal M. White Hawk is an attorney advocating on behalf of tribes, an enrolled member of the Rosebud Sioux Tribe of South Dakota, and a graduate of the Indian Legal Program at Arizona State University's Sandra Day O'Connor College of Law.

* * *

Between 2006 and 2022, we facilitated sixteen Truth Healing Reconciliation Forums. The responses from adoptees, former fostered individuals, family members, and social service professionals confirm that the process of truth telling and listening begins the process of reconciliation. The forums also serve as a form of education. The lived experiences of adoptees, fostered individuals, and birth relatives demonstrate historical trauma, as their comments show.

Here are some of the post-evaluation responses from various forums.

● "I learned how to pray."
  Foster youth

● "This is the first time I have seen Indian people other than in my office."
  ICWA social worker

● "I learned to support my sister."
  Adoptive sister

● "I listened to an elder talk about [what] going to boarding school was like. It made me sad. But it also gave me hope that if he could survive that, then I should be able to survive foster care."
  Foster youth

● "Being a part of the Native American Fosters/Adoptees' Forum has been like a baptism for my soul. I attended their very first forum and have immense feelings for my culture and my new friends. This is a pilgrimage that every Native American adoptee should consider. We are all in different stages of adoption, but being together helps with the healing and understanding and spreads compassion for our plight."
  Susie Fedorko, adoptee, Grand Portage Band of Ojibwe, Minnesota

● "I went to the gathering because it said healing, and at that time I was in need of some serious spiritual and emotional cleansing. Even though I was not one who had been adopted out, many of the old ones I knew were.

"I didn't feel like I belonged there until the first circle. Mine was mainly social workers and college professors, people with degrees, education, and status with one another, and then there was lil ol' me. It was strange how none of them seemed able to put into words what they were feeling or thinking, but when I summarized what I had heard from them, they were all like, 'Yeah, that's it, yeah, that's what I meant.' So, I did it for them and did the writing, too. One elder man later told me how much he appreciated that and that he thought I was able to read people from their hearts. I denied it and said no, I just listen good, that's all, and he smiled and patted my shoulder and left.

"Another circle I was in was most powerful. Two small brothers who were still in placement told their stories of being taken from their families. Their story of abusive foster homes and what they went through was painful to hear. A white lady social worker was there. She broke down; she cried so hard her shoulders shook. She apologized to the boys although she had not worked with them; she apologized to the ones she had taken from their families. She apologized for not understanding and not listening and just following those policies of her organization. I cried when one of the little boys got up, went to her, put his hand on her shoulder and said it's okay, it isn't your fault, and he allowed her to hug him. The strength of spirit that little one possessed amazed me. He was so small in physical form but mighty and pure in spiritual form. As she held him, she said she would do things differently. I hope she did and is still doing it.

"I remember how I felt when the elder Chris Leith wiped me down with his fan. As he did, I told myself to 'let it go, let it go,' and 'open your mind.' . . . I prayed also for the ones who carried pain that they, too, would be able to open up and allow it to leave when that fan touched them.

"When we all held the four direction hoop rope, it felt like there was a force holding the rope, and that it was actually holding us up. I think it was that, yes, we all came there with our own agendas, our own issues, our own preconceived ideas, our own baggage and hurt, but when we held that rope, we were of one mind with one vision and hope in our vision of healing— and as that rope felt to be holding us up, it was actually us holding up one another. We were unified in spirit and that vision.

"That's where we need to be, huh? We need to be willing to hold others up in their times of need.

"Gigawaabamin minawaa."

Esther Humphrey, Leech Lake Band of Ojibwe

● "Sandy White Hawk provides healing forums for First Nations adoptees that address the unique needs of Native adopted and fostered persons. Non-native persons who respectfully attend such gatherings also receive support and reconciliation as they share the common experience of adoption. Sandy White Hawk's groundbreaking work helps all who have been impacted by adoption to address the past and find peace for the present and the future. For child welfare professionals, the forums are essential to ensuring best practices and to ethical policies."

Mary Martin Mason, former director, Minnesota Adoption Resource Network

● "The first time I attended a forum, I was a director at a nonprofit organization that licensed foster homes in four states, including Minnesota. My initial expectation of the event was that there would probably be very heartfelt and moving presentations from Native American individuals who have experienced out-of-home placements in their youth. I comfortably sat back in my chair and prepared to follow someone else on their journey into the past. However, little did I know that I would move from my comfortable seat as an observer and explore my own journey as a child welfare professional.

"I realized that I was a participant in the victories and the heartaches that others attach to the entities we label as child welfare/protection institutions. It is very challenging as an administrator to accept the blame for all of the hurtful things that were historically imposed on Native American peoples in the name of helping. I was not born when many of the oppressive and near genocidal assaults on Indian nations occurred. While I did not participate in those events, I listened to those who related what was left behind after Native American children were removed from their families and communities and placed in boarding schools or adopted into unloving, trauma-ridden environments. The trauma and abuse they experienced as a result of child welfare/protection institutions has left an open sore within the hearts of many. That wound was passed down from generation to generation. I believe the forum provided an environment for those who were hurt by the system to share their story with individuals who have the propensity to make changes.

"While I was not a part of the horrendous acts inflicted on Indian children in a historical sense, I am still a representative of the institution that did. When I stand before the communities that we serve, I am the embodiment of the child welfare institution—past, present, and future. The forum provided space for me to share the heavy burden and responsibility I have assumed as an administrator in this institution. As an administrator I, too, had a story to tell, and I believe the forum provided level ground for all concerned to share and begin dialogues for healing."

Lynn Lewis, former Hennepin County Child Protection Manager, Minneapolis

● "This will forever change how I advocate for Indian children."
A guardian ad litem at the first forum

● "My experience was amazing, at times sad, always poignant, and very inspiring! On a personal level, to feel the strength, love, and values of the people who shared their journeys brought a mix of sadness for the losses they shared and inspiration in learning of the healing they worked hard to experience. As the adoptive parent of a Native child, it helped me to put into perspective some of what life was probably like for his birth mother and her family. She lived part of her life on a reservation and part off. Because she was deep into her alcoholism, Maine Department of Health and Human Services had taken two of her three children. She passed away when still very young. If another such forum was to take place in Old Town, I would encourage my son, who is now thirty, to attend as well. I am convinced he would benefit from that type of closure and/or involvement that he has never had.

"On a professional level, the experience was a bit awkward, yet necessary. I provide support services to foster, adoptive, and kinship parents. Two of my clients were in attendance, both wanting the same Native child. That experience gave me a lot to think about in terms of the need to see the whole picture as viewed by biological family and foster family. I strongly believe that empathy is key to nearly all the work I do, yet helping individuals see the value in collaborating is often a struggle, especially when one family thinks they are more appropriate to parent than another. That is also a simple, true fact—but no less painful for the one who does not get to parent. (Complicated stuff!) Sadly, the family that stood to benefit the most was unable to stay for the amazing event and left in tears. I hope someday she and her entire family will participate. She was simply too fragile and vulnerable on that day. Understand that is my opinion, and perhaps not the way she viewed the circumstances.

"I absolutely recommend this event to anyone working with families, Native or otherwise, and certainly to professionals who need to understand the power of Native American cultures and identity in our work. Preserving and respecting the culture, values, and strengths of each tribe and person is preserving America's history! That people walk away feeling more peaceful and valued, no matter their heritage, is another plus provided by the repatriation."

Bette Hoxie, executive director of Adoptive and Foster Families of Maine

● "I was impressed with the truly cross-cultural application of the healing ceremony model. The day and hands-on exercises put me in touch first with ALL of my feelings and experiences as a parent, kin, and adoptive parent. I was also aware of the relevance as a social worker and administrator in this field."

Tim Plant, Licensed Independent Clinical Social Worker, MBA

The sharing at talking circles is a constant source of support, community, and welcome.

● "I enjoy the monthly talking circle/potluck because it is a chance for me to meet other adoptees and foster youth who know what it's like to wonder about who they are and where they come from. A lot of times, I don't feel quite at home in the larger Indian community, but the talking circle honors my experience as an adoptee, and I feel accepted in a way that just isn't possible in the larger community."

Joseph Rasmussen, "Mishquaanaquad," Minnesota adoptee of Red Lake Ojibwe and Canadian Métis descent (Migizi Dodem)

● "I have been attending the adoptee potluck and talking circles for a few years now. I find them extremely helpful and hopeful to me personally, as well as to those that attend. It is a way to meet, share our stories and heal, and grow from the lives we have all shared as Native adoptees. I like meeting the folks that attend; each person gives so much to others in talking about their experiences, strength, and hope for bettering their lives with living in two worlds. I feel that it is easier to be open and express myself, because everyone there is in your same situation. Sandy has been significant in my healing and in my journey coming back to the community. She gives a warm, kind hand—one of strength and support that builds the bridge—and encourages us all to see the possibility of connecting to our culture and community. Sandy has been very, very instrumental in the work that she does for the whole community. Her vision, steadfastness, and grace have made it possible for many adoptees to return to their culture."

Claudia Foussard, adoptee

● "The talking circle gives me the chance to deeply understand the complexities of adoptees' personal histories and current lives. I love hearing from a variety of individuals about whatever is on their mind; it is a wonderful opportunity for deep connection as well as learning from others' hard-won insights."

Carolyn Liebler, adoptive sister of a Native person

● "I like to offer help to the person who is speaking for the first time and tell them, 'You close one door and open yet another.' I feel good when I leave, because maybe we gave that person a hand in their walk."

Nelson Fox, adoptee from Canada

● "The hole in my heart is beginning to be filled by the love and sharing of the healing friends that are in our circle. Before the circle, I did not allow myself to talk openly about my son, who was adopted at birth. I did not share anything with family or friends for forty-one years. We share our feelings and thoughts without shame or blame, and that is an enormous blessing of safety for such delicate and raw emotions. Thanks to Sandy and all who sit in our circle."

Sharyn Whiterabbit, Ho-Chunk, birth mother

14

Repatriation

WHEN WE COME BACK, the excitement of reconnection carries us. But then the reliving of the removal comes to the surface. The pain of coming back mirrors the pain of when we were taken. Our relatives often think we had a really good life, that we had money, opportunity. But the communities we return to don't understand that many of us were raised in abuse, poverty, extreme emotional isolation, and estrangement from our own adoptive families—families that didn't know us and didn't want to know us.

Because we were raised in white society, adoptees don't know the cultural norms. We can be loud and pushy—or too afraid to speak. We unknowingly often offend our families, especially our elders. Adoptees can bombard with questions. We may want information, ways of knowing who we are, sacred things, but we do not know how to ask respectfully. Indian families are often at a loss on how to correct us, how to teach returning adult relatives what every child in the culture learns: how to communicate. When Native families don't know how to correct those who return, they may just not want to interact with them. There's a lot of miscommunication. But what's sad is that both sides want that relationship. They just don't know how to have it.

Finding that relationship, reconciling, is the work, and it is crucial. Chris and I didn't much discuss the phrase Wicoicage aki un kupi—Generation after generation we are coming home—after we came up with it. We didn't need to. We saw the spiritual concept of Wicoicage—generation after generation—all the time in our people, through the stories of those coming home, hearing how a relative prayed for their return as their ancestors had prayed for the return of those first children, taken away to boarding school.

Now as we work in the forums and see adoptees make it to the powwows, we have begun to understand this phrase in a deeper manner.

The woman choked as the rush of hurt and isolation, dammed up for years, pushed through and into the phone, and the words came from deep within her heart: "I just want to be welcomed by my tribe. I want to be enrolled. I know who my dad is. I have been to the reservation. All my family there accepts me, tells me they love me, and I feel their love and love them. But the tribe says I am not one of them. And why do I feel like a ten-year-old child? All these feelings come back of me not wanting to be dark. I wanted lighter skin. I hated that I was different."

I listened as she sobbed and then apologized for her emotional expression. When she finished, I said, "You *are* ten years old—in your emotions. No one was able to tell you when you were ten why you felt so isolated and confused. You couldn't tell anyone because you had no language to describe it. But you can nurture your heart that was hurt when you were ten. You can tell your ten-year-old heart that the paper you think will make you Indian is a lie. What makes you Indian is who you were born to. You are not that enrollment card. You are your father's and mother's daughter who was loved. They thought of you every year after they were forced to give you up. You are from that land; your DNA is in the land where your ancestors come from. That enrollment card was never how we identified ourselves as Indian people. We defined ourselves by who our parents were, and their parents, and what people and region we came from. That's who you are. The issue of enrollment can be addressed, but don't confuse it with your identity.

"Your identity is in your heart and the hearts of your family. That enrollment system never belonged to us. It causes a lot of hardship, and yet is often the only way for us to keep our land and get the government funding for programs. The enrollment card is not who you are. It is just a piece of paper. I know it will take time to process and grieve, but don't give it your power as an Indian woman."

I have many phone calls like this. Adoptees start telling their stories and apologize if they begin to cry. Often they will say, "I know I shouldn't feel this way. But I feel so crazy at times." I help them see that they have lived in emotional isolation for so many years, and that although they are now starting to come out of it by talking, there just hasn't been a language to say, "I felt so alone, even though I know my adoptive parents loved me."

I explain that their parents did not have to live with different-colored skin and did not have to experience not looking like those around them. There was nothing in their lived experience to relate or understand, even though they may have been sympathetic. Society at large has been influenced by an adoption narrative that is based in the thought that as long as a child is loved, the transracial experience will not affect them. Society at large is also ignoring the racism that permeates American culture and the harms it inflicts on children who are growing up outside the protection of those who have also experienced those assaults. And nobody seems to have the words for the troubled, hurt, confused, or angry adopted child.

Some adoptees will never walk the homeland of their ancestors. Vital information is lost in records that are incomplete or altered, not reported by one of the birth parents, or sealed forever by law. This is a hard uncertainty to carry in one's spirit and heart.

All adoptees carry the blood of their ancestors. Our old people have said that if there is only one drop of Indian blood in someone, they are Indian. Indian people never defined themselves by what we use today, blood quantum.

"No other racial group in America requires its members to prove themselves with blood quantum, yet Indians are often asked how much Indian blood they carry," said Native American journalist and Shoshone-Bannock tribal member Mark Trahant. "American Indians and show dogs are quantified that way. It's a very offensive question, and the answers aren't even valid. Even if someone has a high blood degree, that assumes the records are right, and we know they aren't."*

Blood quantum is a measure of "Indian blood," calculated by looking at one's ancestors. The figures are based on records created after the passage of the Dawes Act of 1887, which supposedly protected Indian property rights by violating treaties, granting land to families that registered under the act, and selling off the "surplus" land. White people decided who was "full blooded" by looking at facial features and hair and scratching skin. Corrupt federal officials manipulated the rolls.

"Say a person owned land the railroad wanted—well, that person's quantum would be lowered," Trahant said. "So much of Indian policy was designed in the 19th century with the thought that Indians would go away. Now, two centuries later, it's become much more complicated because they didn't disappear."

We didn't disappear. Generation after generation, we are coming home.

---

*Here and below, quoted in *Lewistown (Idaho) Tribune*, February 4, 2003.

15

Finding Our Place in the Circle

There is an outside and inside to a circle,
an outside and inside of the self.
There is an outside and inside of the heart,
an outside and inside of a community.

As Indian people, we believe we are all part of the Sacred Circle
    of Life
that knows no beginning and no end,
and when we are gathered in a circle, we are quieted and know
    we are home.
A sacred energy connects us in this circle of life.
It is our relatives, the oyate—the people.

Adoptees grow up outside this Sacred Circle of Life,
far away from this knowledge and understanding.
We stand outside this circle, watching our relatives in sadness,
    not knowing we can move to the inside.
We can't see there is a place waiting for us.
A space that was left when we were taken.

For us, there is yet another circle,
a dark circle of shame, sadness, and discomfort,
a circle so dark we often don't move through it the first time we
    experience it.
We stand frozen and overwhelmed, disconnected from the
    inside, disconnected from where our life began.

*We are disconnected from ourselves by having lived "as if we
    fit in."
The connection of the self is
a biological mirror.
The biological mirror is our people, our relatives.*

*It is healing to see our image reflected to us in a circle of
    people.
The connection from the
outside to the inside of the heart
is the drum, our songs,
our ceremonies.
Our relatives.
Ourselves.*

*Let us help each other with compassion to know this sacred
    truth.*

CHRIS TAUGHT ME to always go to the grassroots people to
share ideas for healing and growth. "If the grassroots people see what you're doing is going to be good for our people,
they'll support it, and you'll know to keep going."

In a colonized way of thinking, some may think there is an
"office" where you take an idea for implementation. That's
what I knew, having grown up in the white world. In Indian
Country, our "offices" are elder's tables and traditional gatherings. We share coffee, a meal, good stories, and thoughts of
what can bring good energy to our people. Our "experts" are
our language speakers who know the value behind the word.
Lakota is a descriptive language based in values. The right
word can bring a vision to life, as it did with Chris mentoring
me. I watched; I listened.

He's been gone since 2011. I still can hear his voice, his
encouragement, his wisdom. Some of the lessons he tried to
teach me I am just now understanding at a deeper level.

One day I said to Chris, "I should go back to school. I could

Chris and I prepare for a ceremony to welcome adoptees at a gathering at Lac du Flambeau.

create my own degree and we could develop a more Indian approach to addressing the issues in adoption."

He told me, "No, that's not a good idea."

I thought, *What, why is he saying this? I know he encourages many to get a degree. Why not me?*

Then he said, "You are so institutionalized I can hardly work with you." I was stunned. What did he mean? I didn't even ask. Maybe I didn't want to know what he meant.

Today I understand. He wanted me to trust ceremony over anything else. To develop an unwavering faith in our way of life. He didn't want me to get sidetracked with essays, research papers, and grades. He wanted my energy in the community, watching and learning. He wanted me to see that language heals. He wanted me to dismantle the white way of thinking, the only thing I understood because of my experience. He wanted me to know that healing is *not* about me. That it is only the Creator who touches the people's minds, body, and spirit and heals them.

Once, on the way home from a ceremony, after an incredible time of healing at a gathering, later in the night he said to me, "Don't let this go to your head. This is nothing to play with." He wanted me to know that we as humans are pitiful, prone to ego and status seeking. As humans, we like to be recognized for our accomplishments. It's fine to feel healthy pride in good work. It's just that as humans, we are weak and fall so easily into an unhealthy pride. He didn't want that for me.

Chris was an incredible healer, with gifts he never talked about. I'd ask him about something someone else had told me that he could do, and he'd give a small grin and say, "No, I don't know why people say I can do that. I can't do that. It's the people—when they come together and believe. It's not me."

He wanted me to know that our ancestors had prayed for us and are waiting for us to live in those prayers, to bring about what could not happen during those times of heavy oppression.

I am so very grateful that in my immature mind I listened to Chris. That I didn't say, "Forget you, old man. I'm going to school." I don't regret it. What I learned would fit on a seed. Yet I did learn, and I value that learning as much now as I used to think I'd value a PhD.

I am not disparaging academia. In fact, this was another vision I had: demonstrating through sound research that adoption of Native American children is a high-risk factor for mental health issues. The First Nations Repatriation Institute has a research team and has published five papers.

In 2012, there still was no large-scale study done on Native American adoptees. Five small studies had been made; the largest interviewed only twenty people. While the studies had great information in them, they didn't seem to be able to help us in court. I reached out to the University of Minnesota and recruited interested parties to form a research team. I wanted to have at least one hundred adoptees answer our survey questions.

The study "American Indian and White Adoptees: Are There Mental Health Differences?" provides clear evidence of the harms.* Respondents included three hundred thirty-six US adoptees and former fostered individuals of all races. Of the one hundred twenty-nine who identified as American Indian, ninety-five said they were reunited with a member of their birth family; their average age was fifty years old, most respondents were women, most had some college education, and the average income was over $55,000.

I had been hearing about adoptee experiences for years, and most of them ranged from difficult to tragic. I heard more abuse stories than I did nurturing stories. Yet, when I saw the numbers, I was so angry.

24 percent experienced sexual abuse

46 percent experienced physical abuse

49 percent experienced emotional abuse

51 percent sought mental therapy for emotional, physical, and sexual abuse

84.5 percent experienced depression

By 2022, "American Indian and White Adoptees: Are There Mental Health Differences?" was still the largest study ever

---

*Ashley L. Landers, Sharon M. Danes, Kate Ingalls-Maloney, and Sandy White Hawk, "American Indian and White Adoptees: Are There Mental Health Differences?," *American Indian and Alaska Native Mental Health Research* 24 (2017): 54–75.

made on Native American adoptees. Our study was used to defend a decision in an Indian child welfare case decided by the supreme court of the state of Washington. Judge Raquel Montoya-Lewis wrote, "In Native American communities across the country, many families tell stories of family members they have lost to the systems of child welfare, adoption, boarding schools, and other institutions that separated Native children from their families and tribes. This history is a living part of tribal communities, with scars that stretch from the earliest days of this country to its most recent ones."*

Clearly, the "safety" of adoption is a myth. Native American adoptees who are raised outside of their communities and outside of their cultures pay a heavy price. Their sense of well-being, their sense of belonging, their self-esteem, and their overall safety were compromised by adoption.

It can seem that a family in crisis will not be able to bounce back to balance. But we need to allow more time. There is no guarantee that life will be better in adoption than it is with a family in crisis. But adoptive families have crises, too, and adoptees are likely to suffer more in the adoptive family than they would in their biological family. There is no "genetic juice" to help them stick together. Over and over, I have stories of adoptees who got the short end of support and nurturing. And if the adoptee was the cause of the family crisis, the adoptee was often kicked out of the family.

Right now, social work professionals have a focus on trauma informed resources for families in trouble. This is a good shift, accessing the backgrounds of parents to help address wounds they may not even know are affecting their life.

But I would like to use *healing* informed resources. What is healing? Encouraging words. Grace in understanding that growth is often two steps forward, one step back. A healing

---

*The court case is In re Dependency of Z.J.G. & M.E.J.G, No. 98003–9, filed September 3, 2020; Department of Children, Youth & Families v. Greer (In re Dependency of Z.J.G.) (Wash. 2020).

informed approach understands this and knows that healing doesn't have a timeline. Yet we can focus the family on stabilizing so their children are not permanently removed. I haven't known a family that wants their children taken from them because they want to use drugs. Most are filled with shame about their behavior. A healing approach would not use phrases like "Chose your children. Not drugs." A healing approach would recognize addiction as the illness that it is. The very core understanding of addiction is that one loses their ability to make a logical decision. An informed intervention can often get through, but anything that creates defensiveness is not helpful.

I guess what I am trying to say is this: We need to work so very hard to avoid adoption. It is clearly not a *better* option and certainly not a guaranteed *safe* option. It is, in fact, the *least desirable of all the options.* Even in the best circumstance, adoption brings trauma that is not part of adoption education. Adoptive parents need to be taught that your child will feel the trauma of being separated from their mother, who carried them for nine months. And when they get older, they will most likely want to know who they are and where they come from. This is normal. They deserve to see who they look like, sound like, walk like. They deserve to hear their birth story. And it is the basic human right for adoptees to have all their birth information.

We need to work so very hard to avoid adoption. Family preservation must be the goal.

I am grateful to have learned to always go first to our communities, where all our wisdom and lessons live. I am also grateful to have found academic friends who understand the importance of community-based participatory research.

Chris always talked about balance. Balance is everything. I strive for that balance as much as I can in my limited humanity. In my work, the balance of academia and community knowledge will always be how I find ways to demonstrate how adoption and foster care are not the answer for our families in crisis. When I was first working with Chris and Jerry, they would often say, "Speak from your heart." At first, I didn't even know what that meant. In the white world, to speak from your heart means you don't know how to speak "intellectually," so you sound weak and uneducated. And besides, I didn't know my own heart. Eventually, I learned to be vulnerable and share my heart. I know I have spoken true words from my heart when elders tell me they liked what I said. From the heart comes everything. When our minds and our hearts are in balance, we are at our strongest place for creativity and wisdom. What Chris said is true: "Your heart has more wisdom than your mind ever will."

As you read this book, there is an adoptee sitting in fear but longing to look for their Indian family. An Indian mother is needlessly losing permanent custody of her child to adoption. Someone is on a tribal Facebook page asking about relatives. Someone is sending me an email asking where to start looking for their Indian family. A grandparent is staring out a window wondering about their grandchild, wondering who she looks like, if she is safe, praying to get to see her before leaving this realm. And through their prayers, and prayers of those in ceremony, we find our way.

Wicoacage aki un kupe—generation after generation, we are coming home.

Acknowledgments

WHEN I REFLECT ON the influences in my life that brought me to the point of writing this book, I am humbled and overwhelmed with gratitude.

Reconnecting with my Indian family was the beginning of me finding a sense of belonging, especially when Uncle Manfred said, "Come home every Rosebud Fair. That's when family returns to visit." All my mother's Fast Horse relatives have welcomed me, which was so healing. My aunt Cecilia was so very helpful, sharing family history and introducing me to family.

My brother Leonard immediately called me *sister* and opened his heart and family to me. We fulfilled a loss in each other's life. His wife, Sandra, helped me with the process of getting my records from the court. His children—my nieces and nephews—and my extended family all have given me the gift of learning what it means to be a Lakota auntie.

Arvol Looking Horse and Paula Horne introduced me to the deeper understanding of vision and ceremony by inviting me to experience World Peace and Prayer Day. Being with them at various gatherings with Chris Leith was an incredible learning experience that gave me confidence to trust my vision.

The Indian community in Madison gave me and my children our first sense of belonging, of being part of a community. We learned Indian values and cultural protocols at the weekly gatherings at the Wil-Mar Community Center. Each of you contributed to my healing. If we shared a laugh, I thank you for that healing medicine.

The powwow circuit, in particular the traditional powwows in Wisconsin, filled my spirit with acceptance and encouragement to accept myself as I was, healing. By bringing me into the veteran circle, the Oneida Nation Color Guard instilled a pride in my status as a veteran. All the powwow dancers, drummers, and singers: your laughter, stories, and listening filled a void I didn't know I had.

Thank you to the local adoptees/former fostered/birth relatives who have trusted me with the stories of your experiences that helped me put into words our common experiences of loss and grief. I pray our voice helps change the current narrative that adoption is a guaranteed safety plan.

Jerry Dearly gave me a grounding and confidence when I was unsure what to do after Chris Leith left this realm. In all our years of working together, I don't think he ever said *no* when I asked him for help. Jerry always said, "It's your vision. I am just helping you." It feels like so much more than that, Jerry, as you talked me through anxieties and confusions. Thank you for all that you have given me and continue to share.

Thank you to cousin LeMoine LaPointe for believing in me and for modeling how to bring people together for healing.

Thank you to the Twin Cities Indian community for helping me welcome our relatives home at the annual Gathering for Our Children and Returning Adoptees Powwow.

Thank you to Terry Cross and the National Indian Child Welfare Association for giving Chris Leith and me a national platform to share the message that we need to welcome our relatives home. NICWA continues to support the work by giving us space at the annual conference for an adoptee/birth relative/former fostered individual talking circle.

Whenever I was home for Rosebud Fair, I visited relatives and always tried to find Chuck Holquin to update him. In his living room one year, maybe around 1995, he said, "You should write all this down. You should write a book." I smiled and kept talking. It didn't settle into me that I should write a book. What would I write about? Thank you, Chuck, for your kindness and willingness to help me find my family. I will always hold in my heart your words, "Your mother is right here. She's been waiting for you."

In 2008 I got a phone call from a journalist, Chris Graef, who somehow knew of me and said, "You should write a book." I was in the hospital then, but I had started writing and didn't really have a good structure or anyone editing. For a couple of years, Chris helped me with editing and creating structure.

Dr. Priscilla Day (MSW, EdD, and professor emerita, social work) and Judge William Thorne (retired tribal and Utah state court judge) gave me my first professional encouragement. Thank you for encouraging me to use my voice to educate child welfare workers.

There are many others whose names I can't recall who nudged me to put my life into words. To those who encouraged me: you know who you are, and I thank you.

But this book would not have been finished if it were not for Dr. Amy Lonetree, professor of history at University of California, Santa Cruz. I'll always recall her reaction when she read my draft: "This book needs to see the light of day." Amy instilled confidence with her encouragement. Thank you, Amy, for the weekly phone calls that kept me on track to finish—and for the introduction to the Minnesota Historical Society Press. I am happy this book found a publishing home there. Wopila tanka (deep heartfelt thank you), my friend.

Even with all these amazing influences, I still wouldn't have been able to accomplish this without family members who believe in my dreams and visions and encourage me. My husband, George McCauley, has always believed in me.

George is a great listener and has offered me insightful, valuable feedback. His Omaha family, especially his uncle Jeff and his cousin Cyndi, also gave me a sense of belonging. Indians heal each other by just being themselves and seeing each other's strengths.

I am blessed beyond measure.

Appendix 1

Child Welfare League of America 2001 Apology

SHAY BILCHIK
Executive Director
Child Welfare League of America

This apology was delivered as the keynote address at the National Indian Child Welfare Association Conference held in Anchorage, Alaska, in April 2001.

Good morning, ladies and gentlemen, and thank you, Terry, for that gracious introduction. I am honored to have been invited, and honored to address this gathering. I look forward to being with you over the rest of the day and evening, to listening to and with you, and learning from you.

It was a long trip to be here today, for me individually, and for the Child Welfare League of America as an organization— so I am delighted to be able to share some of my thoughts, and reflect on that journey.

Before we get down to business, though, I want to acknowledge your recent loss of a great leader, Eloise King. I did not know her, but my staff who knew her and worked with her have told me what a remarkable and energetic person she was and what an influence she will continue to have. She will live on through all of you.

I. Truth and Reconciliation

I want to begin with a story that was a favorite of Dr. Carlos Montezuma, also known as Wassaja. He was an Indian activist, a Yavapai who was born in 1875 at Fort MacDowell, Arizona, and a physician, back in the days when doctors made house calls. As he told the story, a certain doctor used to walk once a week or so down a particular street to visit a patient. On his way, he passed by the home where a friend of the patient lived. Each time he passed her door on the way back from his house call, she would be sitting outside, and she would ask how her friend was doing. "She's improving," the doctor always reported.

After this had gone on for many weeks, there came a day when he had a different answer: "I'm sorry, she's dead." The woman went inside and conveyed this news to her husband. "What did she die of?" he asked. "I don't know," said the woman. "I guess she died of improvement."

When Carlos Montezuma told this story, sometimes in testifying before Congress about the condition of his people, he used it to warn his audience that American Indians and their irreplaceable cultures were in danger of dying from "improvement" if the US government persisted in the policies it was following.

Now the Child Welfare League of America, the organization I represent, has never been a part of the US government. But most of its members, public and private child welfare organizations, represent a profession that has always been dedicated to improvement, in its positive and sometimes negative sense. For that reason, I think that you and all the people you represent deserve an accounting of one phase of our history.

I have not met many of you before today, and we don't yet have an established relationship. Even so, I want to talk with you on a very personal basis about a matter of great importance to all of us.

The spirit in which I stand before you today, as a representative of CWLA and as an individual, is the spirit of truth and reconciliation. In recent years, many countries have dealt with the aftermath of a period of great injustice by creating national truth commissions. This approach was based in the belief that while the past could not be undone, it could be faced squarely, and in a highly public forum—and that a full accounting of the truth was the best possible basis for moving forward to build the future. When the truth had been told as fully as possible, those who had been offended could at least have the knowledge that denial was at an end, and that the world knew what they had suffered. The perpetrators shared that knowledge. Reparations and reconciliation could proceed, on the foundation of truth.

It is with this attitude that I approach you today, and begin a discussion that I realize will need to continue—and to grow over time.

Some of you are already familiar with CWLA, but for those who are not, I'll offer a brief history. In 1909, the first White House Conference on the Care of Dependent Children recommended the formation of both a Children's Bureau within the federal government and a non-governmental body that would unite the various public and private groups working across the United States for the sake of children and families. Around the same time, leaders of many child-serving organizations in the Eastern and Midwestern states were realizing for themselves that they would be stronger together than alone. They were particularly interested in developing standards to guide child welfare practice, in hopes that high-quality services would become the national norm. CWLA opened its doors in New York City in 1920 with sixty-three member agencies.

This all happened just about the time that child welfare was beginning to take itself seriously as a profession. Individuals viewing the work from something of a business perspective were stepping up to take control away from the "church ladies" and society wives who had originally established many of our agencies, and a few colleges were beginning to offer professional degrees in social work.

Since 1920, CWLA and the child welfare profession have grown up side by side, and although we like to believe that today's practice is the state of the art, we know that both still have a lot of growing to do. In no area of practice is this truer than in Indian Child Welfare.

Our profession is other-centered. It's dedicated to improving conditions of life for people, like children, whose capacity to help themselves is limited by age or other circumstances. By its very nature, this exposes us to a strong temptation to think we know what's best for other people, so we constantly have to rediscover humility and respect.

Although we strive to provide leadership for our member agencies, as a membership organization we haven't usually been very far ahead of our members, who haven't been very far ahead of the mainstream culture. For a long time in the early history of child welfare, many educated middle-class Americans sincerely believed that the world would run smoothly and sweetly if everybody would just make the effort to think and behave like they did. In the name of improvement, Irish and Italian children were scooped up from city tenements that looked crowded and dirty, away from "unfit" single parents and the smells of unfamiliar cooking, taken to the countryside in orphan trains, and parceled out to rural families. Most of them never saw their parents or siblings again.

These were terrible acts, no matter how noble or "professional" the intentions of their perpetrators. Next to the death penalty, the most absolute thing a government can do to an individual is to take a child away. But these were acts against individual immigrant families, and no European national group was singled out for these removals to the point of being imperiled.

One ethnic group, however—American Indians and Alaskan Natives—a people of many cultures and governments, and the original citizens of this land, was singled out for treatment that ranged over the decades from outright massacre to arro-gant and paternalistic "improvement." CWLA played a role in that attempt. We must face this truth.

No matter how well intentioned and how squarely in the mainstream this was at the time, it was wrong; it was hurtful; and it reflected a kind of bias that surfaces feelings of shame, as we look back with the 20/20 vision of hindsight.

I am not here today to deny or minimize that role, but to put it on the table and to acknowledge it as truth. And then, in time, and to the extent that each of us is able, to move forward in a new relationship in which your governments are honored and respected, our actions are based upon your needs and values, and we show proper deference to you in everything that concerns Native children and families.

These are the facts. Between 1958 and 1967, CWLA coop-erated with the Bureau of Indian Affairs, under a federal con-tract, to facilitate an experiment in which 395 Indian children were removed from their tribes and cultures for adoption by non-Indian families. This experiment began primarily in the New England states. CWLA channeled federal funds to its oldest and most established private agencies first, to arrange the adoptions, though public child welfare agencies were also involved toward the end of this period. Exactly 395 adoptions of Indian children were done and studied during this ten-year period, with the numbers peaking in 1967.

ARENA, the Adoption Resource Exchange of North Amer-ica, began in early 1968 as the successor to the BIA/CWLA Indian Adoption Project. Counting the period before 1958 and some years after it, CWLA was partly responsible for approximately 650 children being taken from their tribes and placed in non-Indian homes. For some of you, this story is a part of your personal history.

Through this project, BIA and CWLA actively encouraged states to continue and to expand the practice of "rescuing" Native children from their own culture, from their very fam-ilies. Because of this legitimizing effect, the indirect results of this initiative cannot be measured by the numbers I have cited. Paternalism under the guise of child welfare is still alive in many locations today, as you well know.

Far from the Reservation, David Fanshel's 1972 CWLA study of these adoptions (which only covered five years in the children's lives), concluded that while the children were doing well and the adoptive parents were delighted in almost every case, only Indians themselves could ultimately decide whether this adoption program should continue. "It is my belief," Fanshel wrote, "that only the Indian people have the right to determine whether their children can be placed in white homes."

Indian people knew from the beginning that this policy was very wrong. In Fanshel's own words, they saw this "as the ultimate indignity that has been inflicted upon them."

Fanshel came to this realization, as he concluded his research, because of the vigorous Indian activism that was underway in the early 1970s. Your legislative answer, after another five or six years of education and advocacy, was the Indian Child Welfare Act, passed into law in 1978. In the words of ICWA, Congress endorsed the unassailable fact that "no resource is more vital to the continued existence and integrity of Indian tribes than their children." As you have clearly articulated, children are the future.

While adoption was not as wholesale as the infamous Indian schools, in terms of lost heritage, it was even more absolute. I deeply regret the fact that CWLA's active participation gave credibility to such a hurtful, biased, and disgraceful course of action. I also acknowledge that a CWLA representative testified against ICWA at least once, although fortunately, that testimony did not achieve its end.

As we look at these events with today's perspective, we see them as both catastrophic and unforgivable. Speaking for CWLA and its staff, I offer our sincere and deep regret for what preceded us.

The people who make up CWLA today did not commit these wrongs, but we acknowledge that our organization did. They are a matter of record. We acknowledge this inheritance, this legacy of racism and arrogance. And we acknowledge that this legacy makes your work more difficult, every day. As we accept this legacy, we also accept the moral responsibility to move forward in an aggressive, proactive, and positive manner, as we pledge ourselves to see that nothing like what has happened ever happens again. And we can ask—I do ask and hope—for a chance to earn your respect and to work with you as partners, on the basis of truth, on the ground of our common commitment to the well-being of children and young people and the integrity of families and cultures.

We will begin by demonstrating our respect for you and your work, recognizing the authority of your governments, and taking seriously our position of influence with public and private child welfare agencies and the governments supporting them, to fully comply with the spirit and the letter of the Act.

In recent decades our relationship has been characterized by a fluctuating level of effort and many sins of omission. There has been silence from the League on many occasions when we should have spoken out, on ICWA in particular. And we haven't yet demonstrated sufficient leadership for our members, or the field, in this area.

But more encouraging things have been happening recently, and the trend is definitely looking up. The credit for that goes largely to Terry Cross, of NICWA and the Seneca Nation, and to Faith Smith, founder and president of Native American Educational Services College, who has served on our board since 1992. Faith Smith is an Ojibwe from the Lac Courte Oreilles in Wisconsin. Both of them have been insistent and persistent—in the friendliest possible way. A newer CWLA Board member, Faith Roessel, who is a Navajo from Round Rock, Arizona, has also guided our new course. And a number of our staff members have urged and guided us in this direction, beginning with Burt Annin in the 1980s and including Deputy Director Shirley Marcus Allen and staff members Linda Spears, Lynda Arnold, John George, Tom Hay, and others. We established an internal Task Force on Indian Child

Welfare in early 1999, and some of the recommendations it has developed are already being implemented.

II. Where CWLA Is Today in This Area

I want to begin by mentioning some of the areas that our Task Force on Indian Child Welfare has identified as necessary and appropriate for collaboration between CWLA and national and tribal organizations that represent the interests of Indian children. The list begins with some groundwork tasks to bring us into readiness for collaboration. Collaboration is probably the most important thing for us to do when it comes to Indian child welfare. We should and will work closely with tribes and Indian organizations, most significantly NICWA. In this way we can strengthen accountability while we work toward better quality services and outcomes.

1. The first (and ongoing) step in our efforts is listening and learning. We are committed to that mode as we move forward, but we may slip back into the old social worker bossiness now and again, so please be prepared to remind us when we need to hush and listen.

Some of you have been the gracious hosts who invited CWLA staff members to visit the reservations and meet with tribal elders and others from whom they can take direction and understanding. Shirley Marcus Allen spent two unforgettable days on the Navajo Nation in December. Chris Gerhard participated in a listening forum in Window Rock, Arizona, in January of this year. Most of the twenty-eight people with whom she met were from the Navajo tribe, but there was one representative each from the Hopi, the Blackfeet tribe in Montana, and the Cherokee Nation in Oklahoma. We had another listening forum during our national conference in February, and I'm looking forward to sitting down with some of you this evening. I know we have some catching up to do, when it comes to listening, but we're making a start.

2. The second step will be educating our board, our staff, and our membership about issues pertinent to the welfare of Indian children. The members of the Task Force who are conducting this formal and informal training all have considerable experience in working collaboratively with tribal child welfare systems. Terry Cross, without realizing it, we are sure, has been considered by our staff as an important informal adviser to this group. One Task Force member, Linda Spears, is a member of the Narragansett Tribe. Linda conducted an all-staff training on Indian child welfare several years ago, and will be repeating it at intervals. Our in-house publications will also play an educational role.

Moving toward the goal of educating our membership, we had three workshops on Indian child welfare at the 2001 national conference in February. Some of you may have facilitated those sessions, served on panels, or otherwise participated. Thirty people saw the film *Return of the Navajo Boy* in a special screening at the national conference. We are planning listening forums and educational sessions for our upcoming regional conferences, including additional showings of the film.

Engaging our membership is an important part of our work in any area, but particularly in relation to Indian child welfare. We understand that we must bring "value added" to this work. For example: helping our members learn how to work more effectively with Indian children and families—enhancing their cultural competence, helping to reinforce the sovereignty of tribes across the country, creating a stronger voice in support of Indian children and families, and simply adding support in areas where we all agree that we have something unique to offer.

3. Beyond our own staff, board, and members, we have a number of collaborative efforts underway. We're working with the Native American Foster Parent Association in Chicago to promote their accreditation, and planning some joint training for foster parents.

We are participating in a series of forums on improving permanency for Indian children and families, with NICWA, the National Resource Center on Foster Care and Permanency Planning, Casey, and the National Indian Children's Alliance. Forums have been held involving the tribes of South Dakota, Alaska, Oregon, Idaho, and Montana, with Arizona coming up next week. Tribal teams submit proposals to participate in these forums, and state representatives also attend so they can improve their practice and support of tribal plans.

We've been including experts from NICWA and other organizations in reviewing and revising our standards for Services to Abused or Neglected Children and Their Families, Adoption, and Kinship Care. And their input is beginning to make its way into the final publications of these standards.

Task Force members are already working with the CWLA membership committee to find better ways to support tribal and urban Indian organizations, in some areas where our working together would be mutually beneficial.

Tom Hay, of our staff, is with us today. Tom is the project manager, working under director Lynda Arnold, of the National Resource Center for Information Technology in Child Welfare. For nearly two years, CWLA and the National Indian Child Welfare Association have been working together around the National Resource Center, which is housed at CWLA and funded by the Children's Bureau of the Department of Health and Human Services. Our partnership began with developing the successful application together. The mandate of the Resource Center includes helping tribes to incorporate information technology and data use into your child welfare services, and helping states to incorporate tribal child welfare issues into their information systems and data use. As part of this work, there is a survey in your conference packets that we will use to better understand tribal information technology needs and challenges. Some preliminary results of this survey are being presented at this conference by Tom and Mary McNevins from NICWA. Please fill out the survey and turn it in, so that together we can find the best ways to use data and technology to help all of our kids and families.

State agency people here in Alaska know how useful this kind of data can be. Before CWLA established the National Data Analysis System, which is an interactive, online collection of child welfare data by state, we published an annual volume of state-by-state statistics called the CWLA Stat Book. The first year the Stat Book came out, its charts and graphs—all based on information provided by the states— showed Alaska with unusually high numbers of child abuse reports. The information made front-page news, and Governor Tony Knowles, who knew how to make lemonade when he saw lemons, took it straight to the state legislature. The next year he came to our national conference in person to thank us. The statistics, and the headlines, helped him secure appropriations to tackle some long-standing problems.

On the public policy front, CWLA has several initiatives in hand that relate to Indian child welfare. First, I want to make an announcement regarding the Tribal Title IV-E bill that NICWA has worked so hard on, which has been introduced by Senator Daschle and others as S. 550. CWLA unequivocally supports this legislation that will allow tribes direct access to IV-E funds, the largest source of federal funding for child welfare services. The bill allows tribes to choose to either receive direct funding or work within the context of cooperative agreements with states, and ensures Indian children the same access to services that other children and families enjoy nationwide. We will be working with NICWA and other advocates to achieve its passage into law. Yesterday we sent a letter to Senator Daschle, the prime sponsor, with our strong endorsement. We also went on record a couple of years ago as supporting New Mexico's waiver for this purpose.

Another one of our main legislative objectives this year is S. 484, the Child Protection/Alcohol and Drug Partnership Act. Our research indicates that addiction is an issue for two-thirds of all the families who come to the attention of the child welfare system, nationwide, but that treatment is only available for about one-third of those who could benefit from it. We know that treatment is effective when it is available and combined with long-term supports. The shortfall comes down to resources, here as in so many areas.

The legislation that we worked with other advocates to draft, and that we are now promoting, includes a 3 to 5 percent set-aside for Indian tribes, out of a total of 1.9 billion over five years.

In sum, today, we oppose legislation that would undercut ICWA, and we will be supporting legislation to strengthen it.

These are all just beginning steps, but they are ways for us to learn, and to build mutual trust. We look forward to many close personal and organizational relationships in the years ahead. Please be patient with us—but not too patient—and continue to give us feedback on how we're doing. And join with us as we work to improve the practice of our member agencies.

III. CWLA Overall

Next let me tell you a little about what we're doing at CWLA today in overall terms. We've recently developed a ten-year Strategic Plan called "Making Children a National Priority."

Do we think we're going to accomplish that in ten years? Not really. We know that we, and our field, still have a lot to learn. We also know, after all those years, that success doesn't come easily. But to make our children a national priority, we have to periodically re-examine and redefine our goals; we have to build on what we have learned; and we have to keep broadening our base. We have to build critical mass on children's issues, and we'll do that by building relationships.

The Strategic Plan we are now implementing has three key elements related to those three tasks: a National Framework, a Research to Practice Initiative, and Strategic Partnerships.

If you would like a copy of this plan, let Terry or our CWLA staff know, and we will get it to you.

The first, the National Framework, is a template for redefining our national priorities. It will shape CWLA's efforts on the national, state, and community levels, and in the many environments within each community where children, young people, and families live and thrive—or fail to thrive. It delineates the full array of supports and services that families need. Though we've seen it differently in different eras, and we've put it in fresh words for today, the goal of our National Framework is the goal that has united CWLA since 1920: to reduce the victimization and enhance the well-being of all of America's children and youth. We mean it this time, and you can hold us accountable to it by working together with us toward that end.

Most important, it will be a fundamental statement of values, expectations, and objectives for the entire country on behalf of its children and youth, with particular emphasis on the most vulnerable. Both the process of developing it and the dissemination process we go through afterwards will build a consensus on what America owes to its children and families. It's the WHAT of our strategic plan.

In the process of developing this plan, we're inviting input from all the individuals and groups who share the commitment—at least all of those we can reach. CWLA's website, at www.cwla.org, has a link on the left side headed National Framework Survey. If you're online, you can use that to give us your input. We also have a good stack of copies here in the hall.

It's a thin orange booklet called Building Consensus. Our publications department made it into something very beautiful and finished-looking for our national conference, but it really is still a work in progress. We welcome your comments and suggestions. If you don't have a chance to talk to me today, you can talk to John George, from our National Center for Consultation and Professional Development, or Tom Hay, from the National Resource Center for Child Welfare

Information Technology, who are both here today and for the rest of the conference. You can also call Linda Spears, who drafted the document, and whose phone number is inside the back cover.

The second element of CWLA's Strategic Plan is Taking Research to Practice. The challenges our children and our communities face are many and complex, but by and large, they are not new. And they can be solved. For any challenge we can name, there is a tribe or community somewhere in this vast, resourceful country that is implementing a solution.

Now some of these solutions are proven, through solid research; some are promising, though not yet adequately documented or tested; and some are just bright ideas that deserve to be tested. Our tasks are, first, to decide which is which; then to apply research to increase the inventory of proven programs; and finally, to leverage the resources to bring those proven approaches to large-scale implementation. It's the HOW of our plan, and it's an ambitious agenda requiring many hearts, minds, and hands. That's why we need to bring many more people and institutions on board.

Relationships are the key to resources. And resources are the answer to the next question: WITH WHAT? How do we pay for it? Since the resource challenge is possibly the most frustrating of all the challenges we face, we come to the third element of our plan, Building Strategic Relationships. Once we have identified the laws, resources, and infrastructure supports that it will take to bring our combined best efforts to every child who needs them at the community level, we still have a huge gap to close. We have to see that every child, every young person, and every family gets the right supports and services, in the right mix, at the right time, in sufficient duration and sufficient intensity to meet their needs. To do that will take all of us working together—and all the friends we can get.

And it will, of course, take work that honors tribes and finds ways to build the capacity of tribes and Indian organizations to provide services.

IV. Collaborative Models

That brings us back to one of the main themes of this conference: Collaboration! At CWLA, we're constantly forging new alliances and strengthening old ones. Partnerships across the lines between child welfare and juvenile justice, between education and mental health, between juvenile justice and behavioral health, between parents' advocacy organizations and national professional organizations, are building critical mass and strengthening our common advocacy position. They're also straining our staff, but we have to keep building! We need to tighten the weave and thicken the web of interconnections even further, bringing in elected officials and the media and still other partners we probably haven't even thought of yet, before we can get where we need to go.

I know that your program includes sessions on state and tribal collaboration—government to government collaboration with Alaska as one example—and on cross-systems collaboration, of the kind I just referred to. Every one of these is tremendously important for all of us. Before I conclude this portion of my presentation, I want to throw out just a few examples of collaboration models that have made a particular impression on me.

Perhaps since my own experience has brought me from juvenile justice to child welfare, I'm especially aware of models of collaboration across systems. Whether these originate in child welfare, juvenile justice, law enforcement, health, mental health, or education, they succeed by involving several or all of the other systems. Children live their lives in many domains—family, peer group, community, and school—and the best programs reflect that reality. They recognize and touch those many domains.

The juvenile justice system has originated a number of collaborative projects at the national level. My old agency, the Office of Juvenile Justice and Delinquency Prevention, has a new project on Indian youth gangs and a somewhat more established Tribal Youth Project, which has launched part-nerships in Michigan, Arizona, California, and Wisconsin. Partners include five Michigan tribes, the Michigan Public Health Institute, the Native American Institute, Michigan State University at East Lansing, New Mexico State University, the Navajo Nation, and the College of Menominee Nation in Keshena, Wisconsin. Watch the Federal Register for Department of Justice grant announcements. You may see some excellent opportunities.

Some of the best cross-systems partnerships have started out in the mental health system. Alaska was home to one of the pioneering models: the Alaska Youth Initiative. The principles and concepts behind this model were actually borrowed from traditional practices in Indian country.

As I understand it, the Alaska Youth Initiative began in 1985 because of a budget crunch. The state could no longer afford to meet young people's severe social services, mental health, or educational needs by keeping them in out-of-state placements, so administrators began looking around for a way to bring them home. They learned about a new model called "wraparound" (you would know about this), which began by moving children from large residential settings to small ones, but quickly evolved to a model of coordinated, intensive services that allowed them to remain home. With funding from the National Institute of Mental Health and a team approach that brought all the systems together, the state developed individualized plans. In time, almost all of the young people—most of them with very complex needs—were able to return home and remain home. Vermont, Washington State, Idaho, and other states have been inspired to develop their own variations.

The wraparound model, in all of its variations, recognizes parents as the primary authorities on their own children, and puts family members at the center of the team that assesses needs and strengths, then plans and carries out services. In the Hawaii Ohana Project, an offshoot that serves Native Hawaiians on Oahu, family, friends, relatives, neighbors, and other non-professionals must make up at least 51 percent of every team.

The consumers of our services have a valuable perspective to offer, and they're important partners in our work. Unfortunately, their voices are not always heard—at least not in our mainstream, improvement-oriented style of doing social work. That's why it's exciting to see a few practice models gaining ground in the child welfare system that go about things differently.

Family group decision-making is one such model. I said earlier that whatever the challenge is, someone here in the United States is working on a solution. Sometimes, though, we need to look beyond the United States. There's a big world out there. The family group decision-making approach was born in New Zealand, where it was a revolt by the indigenous Maori people against imposed European, expert-driven models. In 1989, it was legislated there as the mandated way to proceed for both child welfare and juvenile justice cases.

Although the child welfare field went to New Zealand to discover family group conferences, I'm sure they're pretty much the way that tribal groups have handled family problems in North America for many generations. It's all about getting everybody at the table and sitting down together to arrive at a solution.

As of 1998, the model was being used in an estimated fifty communities in Colorado, Georgia, Kentucky, Michigan, Minnesota, Montana, New York, North Carolina, Vermont, and Wisconsin. Not all of these are pure models. There's a continuum that runs from paternalism to partnership, and different systems, in adapting the model, have made it to different points along that line. If the family isn't in charge, if its decision can be vetoed, then it's just a case conference: it's not family group decision-making.

When it's done right, it's not about rescuing children from their families: it's about inviting families to claim their own power—and backing them up while they do it. The conference always involves professionals from more than one system, and it always involves more family members than profession-als. Not surprisingly, some professionals are threatened by the shift in power, just as they sometimes are by the active involvement of tribes. But we need to help them get past these feelings because the potential impact of this approach can be so powerful.

Like everything worth doing, this model requires the com-mitment of resources. A coordinator or facilitator plays a key role. In Canada, they estimate that the facilitator—a neutral party who doesn't belong to the family or the system—invests about thirty-six days in preparation alone. All the right people have to be there, and they all have to be prepared. Follow-up is also critical. Families and systems have to deliver what they promise.

The great thing about this model—beyond the fact that it keeps troubled families together and keeps all the family members safe—is that it illustrates the child welfare system's ability to learn from traditional cultures. Yes, we are making some progress in how we work with families, often simply by respecting, listening, and learning.

V. Conclusion

I will leave you with a promise. In a 1999 *Families in Society* article, Terry Cross asked the mainstream child protection field to "honor, endorse, and legitimize tribal efforts in the eyes of funders and policymakers." I enthusiastically accept that challenge, and give you the commitment that CWLA will do our part to make this a reality everywhere in this coun-try. As long as you'll bear in mind that CWLA struggles for the attention of those funders and policymakers too, we will commit to work together, and to approach them as partners at every opportunity.

We want to walk with you, to honor your efforts, to be active in making things right, and to rejoice in your success. And we know that unless you are strong in your efforts to protect and nurture your children, we as a country will never be fully successful.

I know that we still have to prove ourselves as individuals and as an organization, and to demonstrate our commitment through our behavior. We know that reconciliation doesn't happen overnight—it takes time, a lot of discussion, successful experiences, and trust to build into a relationship. But CWLA does have resources to share, in our size, and our influence, and our visibility. And we know that we don't know it all. Let this be the beginning of wisdom.

We know that we need to learn from you what is important and to look to you for leadership as we apply our resources in support of your efforts. Let this be the beginning of a new era for us all.

Appendix 2

The National Congress
of American Indians #SD-02-037

Support for First Nations Orphan Association

WHEREAS, we, the members of the National Congress of American Indians of the United States, invoking the divine blessing of the Creator upon our efforts and purposes, in order to preserve for ourselves and our descendants the inherent sovereign rights of our Indian nations, rights secured under Indian treaties and agreements with the United States, and all other rights and benefits to which we are entitled under the laws and Constitution of the United States, to enlighten the public toward a better understanding of the Indian people and their way of life, to preserve Indian cultural values, and otherwise promote the health, safety and welfare of the Indian people, do hereby establish and submit the following resolution; and

WHEREAS, the National Congress of American Indians (NCAI) was established in 1944 and is the oldest and largest national organization of American Indian and Alaska Native tribal governments; and

WHEREAS, the entire first nations people have been affected by state and private adoption or foster care systems creating post-adoption spiritual and mental health issues, which result in high rates of depression, addiction, school drop out, incarceration and suicide; and

WHEREAS, the federal Indian Child Welfare Act recognizes the need for First Nations people that have been adopted to reconnect with their tribal families and communities and provides for these individuals to have a right to obtain information to help them in this pursuit; and

WHEREAS, state courts and state and private social service agencies are not equipped to address the spiritual, mental health and other special needs of First Nations people that have been adopted; and

WHEREAS, the First Nations Orphan Association goal is to develop strategies that will address post-adoption issues and services to all adoptees, foster care children and families in accordance with our traditional spiritual heritage and the policies of the Indian Child Welfare Act.

NOW THEREFORE BE IT RESOLVED, that the NCAI does hereby support the efforts of the First Nations Orphan Association to develop agencies and services that will address spiritual and advocacy issues affecting adoptees, helping individuals and their families in accordance with our traditional spiritual heritage; and

BE IT FURTHER RESOLVED, that the NCAI supports the First Nations Orphan Association in their efforts to collaborate with Bureau of Indian Affairs Enrollment offices, state and federal offices, tribal enrollment offices, and tribal child welfare programs to disseminate information regarding services that the First Nations Orphan Association provides; and

BE IT FINALLY RESOLVED, that this resolution shall be the policy of NCAI until it is withdrawn or modified by subsequent resolution.

CERTIFICATION:

The foregoing resolution was adopted at the 2002 Annual Session of the National Congress of American Indians, held at the Town and Country Convention Center, in San Diego, California, on November 10–15, 2002, with a quorum present.

Tex Hall, President

ATTEST:

Juana Majel, Recording Secretary

About the Authors

SANDY WHITE HAWK (Sicangu Nation) is the founder of First Nations Repatriation Institute.

GENE THIN ELK (Sicangu Nation) is an internationally known consultant in the area of Indigenous healing methods.

TERRY CROSS (Seneca Nation) is founding executive director of the National Indian Child Welfare Association.